TIME IN, TIME OUT, TIME ENOUGH

A Time Management Guide for Women

Pat Roessle Materka

"I'M NOT WASTING TIME. I'M READING A 'TIME MANAGEMENT' BOOK."

This book is dedicated to Bob, Shannon and Marc.

Library of Congress Cataloging in Publication Data

Materka, Pat Roessle
      Time In, Time Out, Time Enough

Bibliography p. 216
Includes Index
1. Women - Time management. I. Title.
HQ1221.M286   646.7'0088042   92-82944

ISBN 0-9635113-0-0

Second Edition, Copyright ©1993 by Pat Roessle Materka

First Edition, Prentice-Hall, Inc., 1982

Cover design by Karen Cogsdill

Frontpiece cartoon by Harley Schwadron

Excerpt on p. 45 from *Let Us Have Faith* by Helen Keller.
Copyright 1940 by Helen Keller. Reprinted by permission of
Doubleday & Co., Inc.

Published by:

        Time Enough
        1521 Miller Avenue
        Ann Arbor, MI 48103
        (313) 761-5800

CONTENTS

About the Author

Pat Roessle Materka became interested in time management when she was working full-time at the University of Michigan, caring for a house and family, running a weekend antique business, editing a book, serving on several boards and committees and leading a Brownie troop. Rather than quitting the jobs or leaving the house and family, she wrote this book.

Employing its techniques, Pat Materka has gained *Time Enough* to teach over 500 workshops, seminars and short courses on time management and related issues, including *Overcoming Procrastination* and *Shaking the Superwoman Syndrome*. She has been a consultant or keynote speaker for numerous organizations including the American Association of University Women, the League of Women Voters, Michigan Municipal League and the State Bar of Michigan.

She is now an Assistant Director of the University of Michigan Division of Kinesiology and resides with her husband Bob in Ann Arbor, Michigan. She still has not finished cleaning the house.

Introduction to the Introduction

You'd think we'd have learned by now.

It's been 11 years, —*11 years*— since *Time In, Time Out, Time Enough* was first published. Thousands of copies have been sold. You would think we women would finally have our collective act together.

Alas, time management is not a quick fix that is applied once and then lasts forever. It's not like getting your ears pierced. It has to be an ongoing process.

Time management is life management. And life changes. You finally get the hang of your job and the job changes. Your department is reorganized. A new computer system is installed. You get promoted.

Or, you get married. Or divorced. You have a baby. Your last child leaves for college. You enroll in a class, start an exercise program, add on to the house. Each event, minimal or monumental, upsets the balance of your carefully ordered life.

That's why you won't find a one-size-fits-all, ABC formula for time management in this book. Instead, it offers a whole-life approach, with hundreds of strategies you can adopt or adapt right now to your home, work and personal life. For more details, read the rest of the introduction. Better yet, read the book, and don't miss the 150+ tips in the appendix!

The hours you invest in reading this book will pay dividends for the rest of your life. You'll learn ways to do less yet accomplish more, and gain something you may have given up on — time for yourself!

Introduction

This book is for you.

You, who are deftly managing the combined responsibilities of a home, family, and career.

You, who have further complicated your life by enrolling in night school; starting your own business; running for political office; training for the Boston Marathon; raising St. Bernards.

You, at whatever your stage of life: housebound and feeling at loose ends after the birth of your first baby; rising rapidly through the managerial ranks of a large corporation; running a home-catering service to help put three youngsters through college.

You who on some days are a human dynamo, and on others feel frazzled, frenzied, and overwhelmed.

You know that you're active and involved. You are busy from morning until night. But are you getting anything *done*?

Do you set goals for yourself, and meet them? Or can you barely keep up with the demands of everyone else? As you view this mountain of activities are you on top of it? Or trying to tunnel out from under?

Do you keep lists of things to do but keep losing the lists?

Are you better at thinking up reasons to extend deadlines than meeting them?

Do you tend to say "Yes" to committees you have little interest in?

Do you often say "Not now" to your children?

Do you end every day feeling a little bit further behind?

Do you feel that with just two extra hours a day you might have gotten everything accomplished?

You're certainly not alone. I have surveyed and interviewed some 200 women about the ways in which they save and spend their time, and not one of them complained about having too much of it!

Time is an enigma. Everyone has the same amount, it's said, and everyone feels she hasn't enough. Yet everyone has all the time there is.

On the other hand, time is one of the most flexible resources around. It can be stretched, saved, borrowed, bought, wasted, salvaged, created and, above all, *controlled.*

The methods of time management are simple and the rewards are infinite. It is mainly a matter of recognizing and changing troublesome habits, such as putting things off, and adopting healthy new ones, such as planning ahead.

You'll be putting forth less effort, not more, by identifying priorities, consolidating, eliminating, delegating, and saying no. But you'll be accomplishing more by thinking in terms of *objectives* instead of *procedures.* And you won't be doing everything alone. It's far more practical to share responsibilities and resources with your co-workers, family, and friends.

The strategies on these pages can be applied anywhere, from the committee meeting to the supermarket. They are useful when you are under severe pressure to make a decision or finish a project. But they will really pay off during those long stretches of unstructured time when you have lots to do and don't know where to begin.

The first part of the book is aimed at helping you get a handle on how you are using your time now and how to use it better. You will learn:

- How to track your "prime time" and schedule your most demanding activities during those hours when you feel most mentally and physically alert, reserving routine tasks for when your energy level is ebbing.
- How to deal with procrastination, indecisiveness, guilt, and other hangups using a five-step behavioral modification plan.
- How to use the cheap, practical tools of time management such as lists, files, drawers, calendars, clocks, and telephones.

Next we'll move on to all of those areas of your life where the basic principles are applied:

- *Your work life.* Becoming more effective in the office or in running your own business.
- *Your home life.* Organizing your environment. Cutting cleaning, cooking, laundry, shopping, and other maintenance tasks to a minimum.
- *Your family life.* Improving communication and cooperation with those you live with. Ensuring true "quality time" together.
- *Your social life.* Networking, to expedite everyday needs and further career goals. Making time for relaxed, rewarding get-togethers with friends.
- *Your personal life.* Increasing your energy reserves through exercise, nutrition, and rest. Quashing the "Superwoman" image and ferreting out time for yourself alone.

A Woman's Issue

When I set out to write this book, some people asked: Why aim it just at women? Men have the same time-management problems as women.

Not as I see it.

True, we share the same symptoms. Indecisiveness, procrastination, and other forms of wheelspinning are human traits, not female ones.

But the consequences of these behaviors are worse for women, particularly that growing majority of us who work both inside and outside the home. Single, married, or divorced, we put in a sixty-to-eighty-hour work week on the average, leaving little margin for wasted energy and time. A man can bring home a bulging briefcase and catch up on things he didn't finish at the office. A woman who does the same merely doubles her load. There is plenty of work waiting for her at home.

In the 1980s, more than half the eligible United States female population—over 42 million of us—either had a job or were looking for one. This includes three out of five mothers of school-aged children and more than two out of five mothers of preschoolers and infants.

As to future projections, the National Assessment of Educational Progress reported in 1978 that only 3 percent of seventeen-year-old females surveyed across the country picked "housewife" as their first career choice. Young women appear to consider working outside the home almost a certainty.

1

A dual-career marriage can be a demanding commitment, with or without children. But role-sharing looks easy compared to the responsibilities single or divorced women face on their own. Close to 3 million women are working *and* raising families alone, and that figure, like the divorce rate, has been steadily increasing. According to the Bureau of Labor Statistics, these women earn less than half the income averaged by male heads of households.

Add up all a woman's roles and duties, factor in her lower income and her almost invariably higher (if not total) responsibility for child care and housework, divide it by the hours of the day, and you come out with a whopping time and energy deficit.

But you already know this.

And this is not meant to be another diatribe on sexual inequality and injustice.

The vast majority of women I know take on multiple roles willingly. They work hard, they feel tired, and they admit to feeling pulled in seven directions at once. But each sphere of their lives has irresistible challenges and rewards.

The situation can be argued from both sides. Life is unfair because women have so much to do. Life is wonderful because women have so many options.

This book will not dwell on the image of the harried, hurried, overworked, and underappreciated woman of the eighties. Most of us have made a conscious decision to keep our shoulders to the wheel, the home fires burning, the cradle rocking. We believe we can handle it!

We could handle it better, however, if we just had a little more time.

If there weren't so many interruptions.

If we could just get organized.

IF IT WORKED FOR ME...

I was born disorganized, or so I was told by apologetic parents. Like many women, I thought it best to adjust to my limitations rather than try to overcome them. Besides, I had heard that disorganized people were creative, and creativity seemed like an appealing trait. I enjoyed thinking of myself as "creative."

But have you ever tried being creative in a house where every floor, drawer, and countertop is heaped with clutter? I couldn't even find a tool of creativity—eggbeater, crochet hook, or even a working pen—much less a clear surface to write on. My "creative" mind had a hard time with practical matters, such as getting bills paid on time. On the other hand, it was quite inventive thinking up excuses for missing meetings, losing receipts, forgetting at least one essential item on every shopping trip, and putting off unpleasant tasks indefinitely.

Some people procrastinate by not doing anything. My method was to do many things—to take on every activity or responsibility that presented itself. Then, if I was late in finishing a project, or if I decided to scrap it altogether, I had a ready excuse. I was simply so busy.

Ultimately this strategy backfired. By the age of 30 I had acquired several big priorities, any one of which could have filled 12 hours a day. These included a husband; two preschool children, not demanding but dependent; a challenging full-time job in my chosen field; a weekend antique business that was beginning to pay off; and a 120-year-old farmhouse with cobwebs and "character." Each needed lots of attention. None was expendable.

If work expands to fill the time allotted to it, can't the reverse also be true? Can't time expand to accommodate everything you feel is important?

I scurried to the library in search of a book that would revolutionize my life. One that would teach me, in ten easy lessons, how to unclutter, regroup, pare down, and gear up. It didn't exist. I found plenty of self-help books on how to become a more effective executive, a sensuous lover, and a sensitive parent. What was missing was a book that would explain how to make *time* for all these things and still remain human.

The few books I could find on time management focused almost exclusively on office routine and were aimed mostly at men. If the word "she" appeared in the text, it was in reference to the reader's secretary, regarded as one of his "valuable time-saving assets," like his "to do" list. None of the books was addressed to the secretary herself.

None addressed such time-consuming issues as cooking, laundry, and housework. (Why should they? That's what men have wives for.) None even acknowledged the people and events that shoot holes in a woman's day. Errands. Carpools. Repairmen who "Can't say what time I'll be there, lady." Friends who "Just called to say hi!" Husbands who have to be asked. Children who have to be told. Over and over.

Peering beyond the rubble of my immediate surroundings, I could see that many of my female acquaintances seemed to be leading equally frenetic lives. The evidence was hard to conceal; we arrived late to the same events; we seemed to be in a perpetual state of panic and excuse-making.

But there was another group who quite unobtrusively seemed to have everything under control. That is not to say they were all bank vice-presidents who came home, swam thirty laps, popped an oyster souffle into the oven, and set to work making Easter baskets for the hospital children's ward. On the contrary. Their control came from *not* trying to do it all. They set their own priorities and accomplished tasks within that framework. And they didn't fall apart if they fell behind. They were committed but not driven.

So I began collecting information from several sources. Professional time-management experts oriented me to the basics of lists, calendars, file systems, and so on. Busy women and men took time to share their own time problems and solutions. And as I began applying their suggestions in my own life, much of the general chaos seemed to disintegrate.

Writing this book has been a way of putting my own evolving time-management skills to the test. I set daily goals for work on the manuscript, dropped unessential outside commitments, delegated a big share of what I had formerly regarded as "my" housework.

And on days when I made little or no progress, *I didn't feel guilty about it.*

I haven't become a time-management fanatic and I'm not out to make you one. I figure you probably put enough demands on yourself already. But the principles outlined here *can* work for you as they have for me.

None of us has all the answers, and there is no single slick solution that applies to every situation. But there is a lot to be gained from pooling information and resources. Then, with time on your side, you can commit yourself to a course of action. You can reach new levels of accomplishment *and* make things a little easier on yourself.

(2)
Where Does the Time Go?

Remember how the hours dragged when you were a child? They seemed interminable: the minutes until the bell rang for recess. The days left until the weekend. The weeks left until Christmas.

Clocks and calendars seem to gain momentum in adulthood. The years "rush by." "Time flies." And events that occurred long ago "seem like only yesterday."

The sensation adds to a feeling that time is beyond our control. It is as if we are on some high-speed conveyor belt that has jumped its gears and is whizzing us past one event after another. Slow it down? Are you kidding? It's all we can do to hang on!

Time-management problems are not easy to diagnose, especially our own. We tend to blame too much work, too little motivation, an unreasonable boss, or a bad night's sleep. But almost invariably, the source of our problem is a combination of many factors ganging up on us.

This chapter contains several exercises aimed at helping you assess the current demands on your time and your current effectiveness at handling them. You'll also discover why certain activities seem to take far longer than you think they should, and how you can streamline these tasks simply by rearranging or rescheduling them.

GETTING TO KNOW YOU

After you answer the following questions, tuck them away. They may make interesting reading six months from now.

Exercise 1

1. How do you identify yourself (poet, parent, systems analyst, classroom volunteer)? List all your roles and occupations.
2. On a scale of 1 (terrible) to 10 (terrific), how do you rate your present time-management skills?
3. What goals have you set for yourself (a) within six months and (b) within three years?
   Professional goals:
   Family/social goals:
   Personal goals:
4. What have you done *lately* that is related to achieving these goals?
5. What do you enjoy most, and wish you had more time for?
6. Which tasks are you most likely to put off from one day to the next?
7. What would you say are the major constraints on your time management now?
   Within your control:
   Beyond your control:
8. Do you feel you are using your time more productively now than you did five years ago? How and why have your priorities changed?
9. When you feel under pressure, is it most likely to come from:
   Work?
   Meeting family needs?
   Domestic chores?
   Yourself?
10. If you had two free hours today, all to yourself, how would you spend them?

Exercise 2

Getting down to specifics, check your reaction to the following statements.

	YES	NO
1. I make a habit of planning my day and setting goals for what I plan to accomplish.	____	____

2. I often feel I have so many tasks before me that I don't know where to begin.   ____ ____
3. If a task is unpleasant, I just dive in and get it over with.   ____ ____
4. I never write down things I have to do; I just memorize them.   ____ ____
5. I welcome new responsibilities but am careful not to overcommit myself.   ____ ____
6. I often feel I am drowning in paperwork; the top of my desk is buried.   ____ ____
7. When I'm approaching a big deadline, I pace myself by getting a little done each day.   ____ ____
8. I feel guilty about asking someone to do something I am capable of doing myself.   ____ ____
9. When I delegate, I make certain that I am giving out interesting, important tasks, not just busywork.   ____ ____
10. However, I retain authority over the project, and take my share of the credit.   ____ ____
11. I preserve large blocks of uninterrupted time to accomplish important things.   ____ ____
12. I encourage friends to call me at work since I'm often not home in the evening.   ____ ____
13. I try to handle matters with a phone call unless a letter is clearly called for.   ____ ____
14. I keep everything; you never know when it might come in handy.   ____ ____
15. When meetings go off on a tangent, I'm usually the one who reminds participants of the issues at hand.   ____ ____
16. I'm a perfectionist. It doesn't matter how long a job takes as long as it's done right.   ____ ____
17. I rarely worry about past mistakes or future events that are beyond my control.   ____ ____
18. I weigh carefully even the most inconsequential decisions.   ____ ____
19. I habitually set deadlines for myself and for my subordinates.   ____ ____
20. I almost always bring home work from the office, to catch up on.   ____ ____
21. I make sure to spend a certain amount of time daily with each of my children, individually.   ____ ____
22. When I get busy with work, my social life goes right out the window.   ____ ____
23. I put a dollar amount on my time and gladly pay someone to do something I could do myself.   ____ ____

24. I leave things until the last minute on purpose, figuring that I work better under pressure.   ____ ____
25. I always have something with me to work on if I'm stuck in a line or in a waiting room.   ____ ____
26. I make the rounds to several grocery stores each week in search of the best food bargains.   ____ ____
27. I confine my volunteer work to a few causes I really feel strongly about.   ____ ____
28. I feel housework is a woman's responsibility; men have more important things to do.   ____ ____
29. I am careful to get enough sleep each night to be at my best the next day.   ____ ____
30. I'd like to get regular exercise, if only I weren't so busy.   ____ ____

Give yourself 2 points for every odd-numbered statement you marked "yes" and 2 points for every even-numbered statement you marked "no".

If you scored above 50, congratulations! With the strategies outlined in this book, you may be on the verge of moving from excellent to stupendous!

If you scored 40 to 50, you have much of your life well in hand, but a few areas to work on. Now you know what they are.

Scored below 40? Hang in there. There's help in the pages ahead!

It's so easy to take time for granted. What is wasted today will be restored tomorrow, fresh, free, and ours alone. But by the same token, today's hours are irreplaceable. It's more appropriate to treat time as a precious and limited commodity. And as with anything of value, you must be aware of it to appreciate it.

Exercise 3

1. There are 168 hours in a week. How many hours do you estimate that you spend each week on the following?
    (a) Paid work
    (b) Housecleaning
    (c) Child care
    (d) Family activities
    (e) Social contact (including phone calls)
    (f) Sleeping
    (g) Meals (preparation, eating, and cleanup)

(h) Laundry
(i) Shopping (grocery and personal needs)
(j) Miscellaneous errands
(k) Volunteer activities
(l) Meetings (apart from work hours)
(m) Classroom and studying
(n) Hobbies, crafts
(o) Church
(p) Entertainment/recreation
(q) Exercise
(r) Reading
(s) TV watching
(t) Grooming (hair, nails, other)
(u) Commuting
(v) Chauffering children
(w) Daydreaming
(x–z) Other

2. Now rank the top seven of the preceding items in order of their importance to you.

(1)
(2)
(3)
(4)
(5)
(6)
(7)

If you are like many people, you may notice some discrepancies between those things that command most of your time and those you feel are most important. To further clarify your priorities you might make up a list at the end of a typical day of all the things, important and trivial, that demanded your attention. Estimate how long each one took. How long should it have taken?

In the office, for example, do you find yourself frittering away the better part of the morning answering phone calls and opening mail? At home, did watching the late-night rerun of "Lou Grant" do you more good than an extra hour of sleep? And how much time is totally unaccounted for?

What we're looking for here is patterns: Huge amounts of time bestowed on projects that have little long-term value to you; cursory attention to chores that are important but unpleasant. And how many chores are carry-overs from yesterday's agenda? How many have been reslated for tomorrow? Your current time-management habits may be more clearly revealed in what you *avoid* than what you accomplish.

Exercise 4

To really get a handle on your time usage, keep a record of your daily routine for at least two weeks. Carry it with you and faithfully write down everything you do, how many minutes it takes and how you feel (alert, bored, tense, drowsy) while doing it. A simple chart might list the hours (in fifteen-minute segments) vertically, with wide columns for activities and feelings spaced horizontally. In a third column (optional), you might note how much time you feel you *should* have allocated to a given activity.

The process may sound tedious but it works. The method has proven effective in many kinds of behavior-modification programs, the most prominent example being weight control. People who for years have been trying (and failing) to diet are told to write down everything they eat, when they eat, and what kind of mood they are in at the time. Their own records inevitably reveal habits of which they were formerly unconscious: A tendency to snack regularly during certain activities, such as television watching, or when in a certain mood, such as anger or disappointment. A woman is astonished to find that she regularly consumes an entire meal in the process of "tasting" the dishes she is preparing for dinner. A businessman, who takes pride in his ability to skip lunches, learns that he more than makes up for them with the candy bars stashed in his desk drawer. Only after *recognizing* the self-destructive patterns are such people able to take steps to change them.

Your record of activities and time expended should be equally revealing. Several women who made this effort discovered a variety of ways in which they had been spending inappropriate amounts of time. For example:

Ruth noticed that she made a total of eight trips to the supermarket within less than two weeks. "I was trying so hard to economize and buy only the food items we needed immediately, I never planned ahead. Consequently, every other day I had to make a 'quick stop' to buy toilet paper, cat food, or some other indispensable item. I was as-

Time	Activity	Feelings	Comments
7 am	breakfast, kids off to school -	drowsy irritable	overslept
8 -	commuting	alert	
9 -	staff meeting	productive morning	morning seems to be the best part of my day for accomplishing things
10 -	worked on status report		
11 -			
12 -	lunch with friend	okay -	
1 -	contacted clients, set up 3 appointments	too many distractions in office - hard to concentrate	should use this time to clear desk, make calls.
2 -			
3 -		real slump between 3 & 4	
4 -	picked up kids from sitter		dinner is time consuming - the kids don't eat fancy meals - pizza tomorrow!
5 -	dinner		
6 -	running, 30 min.	great! exercise revives me	must get more exercise!
7 -	economics club meeting	should have skipped meeting bored!	
8 -			
9 -	watched tv, read paper		tried to pick up toys, sort laundry. useless at this hour.
10 -	sleep	drained	
11 -			

tounded to find I had devoted nearly five hours one week—counting the time spent driving, parking, and standing in the 'express line'—to purchasing groceries! Now I plan menus on a weekly instead of daily basis and restock items before they run out, not afterward.''

Sandy took a hard look at the ninety minutes a day she was spending commuting to and from work. "I'd considered taking the train when I was first hired, but ruled it out because of the extra expense. Now I realize I'm driving nearly eight hours a week—the equivalent of a working day! I could use that time far more profitably catching up on my reading and paperwork. Besides, the way gas and parking costs have increased, the cost difference is negligible.''

Arlene saw that she was spending more than an hour each evening getting her four-/and six-year-old daughters to bed. "It had become an endless round of orders, pleadings, tantrums, and threats, leaving us all upset and exhausted. Finally I realized that it was taking so long because I was so tired myself at that hour—too tired to argue or enforce my own rules. The girls realized this and pressed their advantage.'' The problem resolved itself when Arlene insisted on baths and pajamas before dinner, and before any games or television. Now the hour before bedtime has become a peaceful period for the family to unwind and relax together.

YOUR ENERGY CYCLE

As Arlene's experience illustrates, the way you feel physically and mentally before you embark on a task is a sure indicator of how long it will take you and how well you will accomplish it. This goes for whatever you're doing, from arbitrating a union settlement to disciplining your children.

Behavioral psychologist Dorothy Tennov defines five capability levels that every person experiences at various times of the day. Level one is peak condition—the period when you are feeling most alert, articulate, and productive. At level two you are competent, but your performance is below optimum. The middle level—level three—is appropriate for performing difficult but familiar tasks, such as typing, filing, and other work-related activities.

Level four is better suited to less demanding routines, including most kinds of light housework. At level five, you can read a novel or take a shower, Tennov says, but it's impossible to learn anything new or do anything creative. The only level lower than five is sleep.[1]

You can define your own capability levels and distinguish for yourself at what points of the day you feel most or least competent. Your stamina will vary from day to day as well as from hour to hour, but after keeping a record for two weeks or so, you should begin to notice a pattern.

Perhaps you thought your energy level was fairly constant: Low when you groggily get dressed in the morning; rising steadily to a moderately high level as you pursue the day's activities; and finally ebbing in the hour or so before you retire to bed. In reality, most people experience a twenty-four-hour cycle of energy peaks, valleys, and plateaus that seem to be based at least partly on their internal biological rhythms. These vary from individual to individual. Thus you might be a "morning person," peppy and alert when you spring out of bed at 5 A.M. but totally exhausted by the dinner hour. Your best friend—if a "night person"—may be able to carry on complex statistical analyses in her laboratory long after midnight but be incapable of even thinking coherently before noon.

You may also notice that you experience a midmorning or midafternoon slump—the precursor to the coffee break—or that you often feel a spurt of energy between about 9 and 11 P.M. each evening. Once you can anticipate these highs and lows, you can use them to your advantage. Simply adjust your activities to correspond to them.

To some extent you probably do this already. When you feel motivated, you take on bigger challenges; when you feel tired, you rest. Yet if you are unaware that your highest capability level generally occurs between, say, 9 A.M. and noon, you run the risk of wasting it. You might fritter away the most productive hours of your day reading the newspaper or chatting on the telephone.

Time is money, right? Think of your twenty-four hours per day as a spending allowance, to be invested in whatever ways offer you the highest return. Your peak energy hours represent a "bonus value" period when your purchasing power is doubled or quadrupled. If the

[1]Adapted from pp. 9-10 in *Super-Self* by Dorothy Tennov. Copyright © 1977 by Dorothy Tennov. Reprinted by permission of Harper & Row, Publishers, Inc. (Funk & Wagnalls) and the author.

local department store offered big discounts and prizes each day between 9 A.M. and noon, you wouldn't want to spend those hours in the parking lot!

Still, your budget is not limitless. You can't "buy out the store." You alone must decide your current needs and how best to spend the time that is your "money."

Your priorities may be expected to change on a daily, even hourly basis. Most days, you will probably reserve your highest energy level for professional endeavors. As an attorney, you will compose your best arguments then. As a musician, you will practice with higher concentration and fewer mistakes.

As an editor working out of your home, you may routinely devote level one to your manuscripts and level three or four to your housework; even level five is adequate for wiping fingerprints off the refrigerator and guiding the vacuum cleaner across the rug.

There is, however, a rationale for tackling your housework at level one. You're in high gear—well organized, committed, buoyant. You will scrub harder and move faster. In short, you will probably accomplish more in an hour at level one than in three hours at level four. If your goal is to minimize the time you spend at housework, this strategy has definite merit.

The basic message is, be flexible. Learn to recognize your energy levels and maneuver your activities so that you can accomplish everything on your agenda, simple and complex. Be aware, of course, that the cycle won't be predictable on a rigid twenty-four-hour basis. Monday mornings may find you drained and disoriented after a particularly lively weekend. At other times, highly motivated and well rested, you can sustain peak condition throughout most of an entire day.

Usually, the greatest difficulty lies not in knowing when you feel competent and industrious, but in knowing when to quit. Many busy people have a tendency to deny fatigue and to push themselves on and on, ever trying to get just one more task accomplished. This ritual is counterproductive. When the figures you're adding start dancing across the columns, when the dinner plates you're stacking seem to weigh twenty pounds apiece, it's time for a break. You'll do the same work in a fraction of the time later on, when you're feeling refreshed.

WHAT TO DO FIRST

Exercise 5

Try classifying your daily activities into those that are most: (1) demanding and important; (2) routine but necessary; (3) worthwhile but not urgent; (4) appropriately delegated; and (5) appropriately reduced or eliminated. Broad categories such as "job" or "housework" won't work here; you must break the categories down into specifics, such as "contacting new clients" or "scouring bathtub." You can begin by ranking the tasks compiled in your two-week activities record.

There are no right or wrong designations. Priorities vary from one person to another, and for each individual, they will vary from day to day. Makeup and grooming may be "routine but necessary" to the average woman, while to a professional model they may be "demanding and important." Polishing silverware may be "demanding and important" (or "appropriately delegated") the day before your relatives arrive for dinner, but may be moved to the bottom of the scale thereafter, or removed from the list entirely.

The intent of this explicit breakdown is to help you identify those functions that are intrinsic to your mental and physical health and to your personal and career goals. It should also put a new perspective on those tasks you have been doing from habit rather than necessity.

Don't be surprised to find little similarity between the activities you claim are most meaningful and the ones that consume most of your time.

One of my highest priorities, for example, is the time I spend with my children. Talking over what happened in school, checking their homework, and hugging them at bedtime are matters I consider extremely important. Housekeeping tasks, on the other hand, are clustered at the bottom of the scale. The only challenge I find in housework lies in discovering ways to minimize it.

About two years ago I noticed that preparing, serving, and particularly cleaning up after dinner were absorbing the greater part of each weekday evening. After work I would pick up the children from the baby-sitter, we would arrive home about six, and the children would plop down in front of the television set while I began fixing the meal. Cooking seemed to help me unwind. Sparing no ingredients or utensils, I managed to clutter up every square inch of countertop in the course of assembling even the simplest salads or casseroles. As a result, the meal was always upstaged by the mess.

Since I'd created the mess, I somehow never expected any help in cleaning it up. While my husband and children read bedtime stories in the living room, I wearily wrapped leftovers and loaded the dishwasher. Sometimes I'd turn on the portable television to relieve the boredom. I could just about finish within the frame of a thirty-minute broadcast; if an hour-long program was scheduled, the cleanup would take me an hour. By then it was the children's bedtime. I had just squandered away three hours—the only three hours we have together on weekdays!

Like most habits, this one was easy to change once recognized. I now prepare two-thirds of the meal the night before, imposing strict limits on the time I use as well as the space. By the next evening, vegetables have been washed and chopped, meats browned and refrigerated. The children set the table while I ready things on the stove, and we all have free time to relax while the food is cooking. I save the more elaborate recipes for weekends, and triple the quantities so that we have a backup supply in the freezer. And the whole family pitches in with the cleanup. All I had to do, it seems, was to ask them.

CHANGING CUSTOMS

Habits are not always so easy to relinquish or change. As with a sturdy pair of boots, it may take years to break them in and make them fit comfortably. We work hard at developing safe, automatic routines to counterbalance the unpredictable and chaotic events in our lives.

Furthermore, good habits save us time. They no longer have to be planned, tested, or evaluated; we can follow them almost unconsciously, assured of dependable results. But habits can outlive their usefulness. They must be periodically evaluated in the context of our changing lives.

While her children were small and dependent, Martha took great satisfaction in the creative aspects of homemaking. She canned peaches, grew roses, and macraméd a seven-foot-square room divider. Her daughters wore hand-smocked pinafores and rarely tasted store-bought bread. Martha never felt bored or dissatisfied.

But by her mid-thirties, with her children in school most of the day, she was ready for a new challenge. She enrolled in some computer programming courses and now works full time for a data-processing firm.

"The hardest adjustment for me was not taking on new responsibilities but putting aside old ones," she relates. "It feels strange to hire someone else to hang wallpaper or to buy ready-made desserts that I used to bake myself. I still enjoy cooking and crafts on occasion, but it's no longer practical to invest several hours or days in those projects. My time is worth more than the money I save.

"I've learned that one can be as creative at a computer terminal as at a sewing machine. Creativity is something you feel, not something you do.

"The only thing uncreative," she concludes thoughtfully, "is failing to try new things."

Maybe you think you haven't time to try anything new. You can barely manage the responsibilities you have now.

Don't worry. Time-management skills develop gradually, not instantaneously. As you build on the ideas and strategies outlined in this book, you will begin to work more methodically and efficiently. You will trim and accelerate the things you *have* to do and gain time for the things you *want* to do. Your steady improvement is simply inevitable.

So get inspired. What kinds of changes do you hope will occur as you begin to bring peace and order to your existence? Will you take on more responsibilities at work? Join in more community or social events? Learn a new sport? Spend more hours with your family? Now is the time to take steps toward meeting these goals.

Suppose that for years you have wanted to try your hand at vegetable gardening, but each spring rolls by and nothing gets planted. This year, do some reading and planning over the winter. Order seeds in February, and dig up the ground after the spring thaw. After this preparation, the actual planting will take less than a morning, and with minimal but regular cultivation, you'll have enough tomatoes in August to bottle your own ketchup!

Similarly, if you want to see changes in your life within the coming year, start *now* to investigate ways to bring them about. If you're considering a career change, begin talking to employment agents, job counselors, and people who work in the fields that interest you. Study the newspaper classified sections; take courses; update your resumé. No project will seem so formidable once you break it into small, manageable tasks and, one by one, dispose of them.

Exercise 6

Here is an easy, rewarding way to prove to yourself that you are not overwhelmed or entrapped by your current obligations. Make a list of all the small but worthwhile things you've been meaning to get around to: A letter or phone call to someone you haven't seen in awhile; the old clothes that have to be sorted out for the church relief drive; the vacation brochures you've meant to send for; the toy you promised to repair. Compile at least twenty ideas, divided when necessary into tasks that can be completed in fifteen to thirty minutes. Include pleasant items as well as tedious ones. (You've probably been putting off many easy, enjoyable chores because you felt guilty about not doing the disagreeable ones.)

Now *commit yourself* to fitting into your routine one new thing each day from the list. Do this new thing in place of the parts of your routine that you recently designated "appropriately reduced or eliminated." Add new "things to do" each week as you think of them, and heap congratulations on yourself as you scratch through those things you've accomplished.

3

Speed Traps

Does this sound like you?

> My overdue book fines could finance a new library wing.
> I just can't turn down a worthy cause.
> My mother would never have used a cake mix.
> It's easier to pick up the crayons myself.
> I'll start my diet tomorrow.
> I work better under pressure.
> I was born this way.

Procrastination, indecisiveness, perfectionism, anxiety, guilt.

They are part of the human condition; behavior patterns so ingrained and familiar you may hardly recognize them as problems.

They seem like such measly little faults. Hardly the caliber of a *real* vice, like hijacking airplanes or setting buildings on fire. But behaviors do not have to be pathological to be destructive. And because they seem inconsequential and commonplace, they slip unnoticed into your daily routine. There, like a band of termites, they chomp away at your control over your life and your time.

Many of these habits took root in your childhood. Your parents and teachers preached perfection. ("If a job is worth doing, it's worth doing right.") Procrastination was your means of rebellion. ("I will do my homework, but not *now*.") You've adapted to your time-wasting tendencies, learned to work around them, and developed an arsenal of imaginative excuses for them. Perhaps you've even convinced yourself that they're endearing. ("Accept me for what I am, everyone...a free spirit.")

19

Instead of accepting and excusing your shortcomings, resolve now to defeat them!

You are not the only one who has to live with them; they inconvenience your family, your co-workers, and your friends. Have you ever planned an outing with a relative who habitually shows up late? Served on a committee with someone who is afraid to take a course of action? Worked for a boss who insists on doing everything her- or himself? It's exasperating enough to put up with this behavior from other people. Why engage in it yourself?

Putting things off, agonizing over decisions, setting impossibly high standards and then feeling guilty for not achieving them—such behavior absorbs energy that could be much more profitably channeled toward *getting things done.* Let's take a closer look at these not-so-harmless hang-ups and how they can be dealt with.

MAYBE...THEN AGAIN...

Indecision can subtract hours from your day and years from your life. It all adds up: The evenings you spend poring over wallpaper books and paint samples; those moments when you pause at the meat counter debating between chicken wings and chuck roast.

To kick the habit of indecisiveness, it is necessary to think in terms of goals, not processes. The sooner you decide to do something, the more time you'll have to enjoy the outcome. If you decide wrong, the more time you'll have to correct the mistake.

Money is the source of many a quandary. The less you have of it the more agonizing the choice. Do you save it or spend; buy now, or wait on the chance that a more desirable price or product will appear later? When you find yourself spending more minutes mulling over a sixty-cent head of lettuce than would be warranted by a 500-share stock transfer, remind yourself that time, too, is money. If you waste the first to save the second, you barely break even.

Of course, some decisions merit a long, thoughtful examination: Moving to a new city, changing jobs, having a baby. These require careful, but not endless, deliberation. Set a time frame for such matters, and use that time for gathering information and advice. In the case of a move to a new city, check into every aspect that is important to you:

Housing costs, school systems, cultural activities, political climate. Learn all you can, weigh the pros and cons, and then decide. Put all doubts behind you. A positive attitude is indispensable to making that decision work!

If it's a decision that affects your staff or your family, by all means consider their viewpoints. A consensus is always more desirable than dictatorship. You'll feel more comfortable as you proceed with their cooperation and support. Sometimes, however, an open invitation for opinions only creates disagreement and protest. If you see conflict brewing, exercise your executive function and announce your course of action with commitment and confidence. Your determination to make a plan work greatly enhances the chances that it *will* work.

In sum, to combat indecisiveness:

- Consider rationally how long this decision should take and give yourself a deadline. Allow several months for choosing a new home; several seconds for choosing which outfit to wear to work in the morning.
- Tell yourself that whatever you decide is only an experiment. Neither the world nor the small part of it that you inhabit will be radically altered if your decision turns out to be a mistake. You can always change your mind.
- Remind yourself that *any* decision is better than no decision. As long as you remain in a quandary, nothing gets done. Take action now and deal with the consequences later.

If you practice being resolute on small matters, such as whether to order the bratwurst or the stuffed shrimp, the dilemma of the vacation versus a new car will seem less overwhelming.

WHAT IF...?

Anxiety is both the cause and effect of indecisiveness. It goes along with a lack of self-confidence, information, money, and other resources, and an excess of work, responsibility, and guilt.

Women who are trying to simultaneously manage a home, a family, and a career—especially those who are single parents—are vulnerable to all kinds of anxieties: "What if little Leo falls out of a tree while he's at the babysitter's?...What if I'm struck by a car while crossing the street and unable to work for six months?...Should I apply for that opening in Personnel? Would it look too pushy? Or should I stay here and ask for a raise?...Did I leave my headlights on in the parking garage? What if the battery is dead?''

Anxiety in mild form is distracting; in extreme cases, immobilizing. Like indecisiveness, it becomes a substitute for action.

Esther was bored and frustrated with her job in a small insurance firm. For most of the day she was alone in the office, typing up form letters on claims adjustments. She had few social contacts and her salary barely covered her living expenses. A new job seemed the obvious solution to her discontent, but Esther was worried. What if her employer found out she was job hunting and decided to fire her? What if she couldn't find a better position? What if she accepted a new job and then couldn't handle it? How would two rapid job changes look on her resumé? The more she analyzed what could go wrong, the less inclined she was to take any chances.

Worrying is not a pleasant pastime, but it is less strenuous than taking risks. By doing nothing, you protect yourself from making a mistake. But you pay a price for playing it safe: You reduce your chance at success.

Anxieties that scramble our attention and block worthwhile goals can be dealt with on both physical and mental levels, says Dr. Chauncey Smith, an Ann Arbor, Michigan, behavioral psychologist.

> The physical symptoms—tense muscles, stomach pains,the jittery feelings—can be reduced through meditation or progressive muscle relaxation. Scientists have shown that you can actually lower your own blood pressure and reduce nervous tension by imagining calm, placid scenes such as waves gently sloshing on a sunlit beach. A commercially produced cassette tape can assist you in teaching yourself progressive muscle relaxation, a technique that has helped people control anxiety and its consequences...from insomnia to stage fright.

> On a cognitive level, anxiety can be reduced by rationally disputing whatever it is that upsets you. . . .Challenge it head on: "Why am I making such a big issue of this? What's the worst thing that could possibly happen if my worries materialize? Would it really be such a catastrophe?"

> Instead of always saying "What if...," practice saying "*so* what if...."

So what if you're rejected or unsuccessful or disappointed? Naturally you will feel frustrated and annoyed, but it is not appropriate or healthy for you to feel devastated.

So what if you're turned down for the loan that you needed for graduate school? So what if the advertising campaign you developed for the firm's biggest account is a bomb? Or the investment you sunk your life savings into goes bankrupt? You'll survive. And the experience, no matter how awful, will make you a stronger and wiser person.

If belittling your worries doesn't help, try blowing them all out of proportion. Worry your head off about all the worst things you can think of: An accident that would leave you in traction for eight weeks; a tax audit; an earthquake; World War III. Now think about how little your worrying will do to deter any of these events. Think back about what worried you most six months or a year ago. Did worrying help then? Did it have any influence on your life as it stands today?

Anxiety crowds out creative, constructive thoughts and prevents us from making the most of what's happening now. The next time your inner voices start chattering about gloom and doom, muzzle them with the following arguments:

- Why am I making such a big issue of this? Is it really that important?
- If the circumstances are beyond my control, worrying will have absolutely no effect except to make me unhappy.
- If the outcome is within my control, why am I not taking action instead of just thinking about it?
- It would be *nice* if things went as I wish; it would be *inconvenient* if they didn't. It wouldn't be *catastrophic*.

IF ONLY...

Guilt is worry in reverse. Instead of addressing the future events we can't change, it focuses on the past things we can't change.

If worrying is unproductive, guilt is even more futile. Worry may at least brace us for a disaster that may happen, and may even alert us so that we can prevent it. Guilt has no redeeming qualities.

"But it keeps us morally upright," some people argue. 'Without guilt, we'd all go around stealing and murdering." Wrong. It's rational thinking that deters us from these actions. We are basically moral people. And as a practical matter, we don't want to get caught or punished. Guilt is nearly always an irrational emotion. It accomplishes nothing.

Women seem to have a penchant for guilt. Those of us who have jobs feel guilty about being unable to drive for the fourth-grade field trip. If we choose to stay home and can vegetables, we feel touchy and defensive about not earning a paycheck. Some women (and men) who have grown comfortable with the image of "poor but struggling" even feel guilty when they achieve success. "Why me? What did I do to deserve this?" they fret. "Am I really good, or was I just lucky? What if I can't live up to everyone's expectations?"

Guilt perpetuates guilt, says Chauncey Smith. "We love to exchange stories about what makes us feel guilty. Talking about guilt is a form of catharsis," he explains. "It invites similar disclosures from our companions, and each new confession is a reassurance that we are, after all, only human."

Teachers, ministers, supervisors, and others in positions of influence are quick to master the manipulative powers of guilt. Advertisers use it to promote every product from air fresheners to disposable diapers. And the people we're closest to—our parents, lovers, and kids—often play on our guilt reserves, even without intending to.

"My son makes me feel so guilty," sighs Brenda, a single parent. "I know he misses having a father around all the time, and he gets bored being with a babysitter after school. I feel I should be taking him to hockey games and horseback riding, but when I get home from work, I have barely enough energy to cook dinner. He seems so lonely sometimes—if only he had a brother or sister for companionship...."

"Understand," Dr. Smith stresses, "that it's not Brenda's son who makes her feel guilty. It's her belief system. She had certain expectations about marriage and family life that have not materialized; an ideal of her behavior as a mother that is not now realistic. She feels guilty because of what she thinks should be happening, not about what is happening."

So the remedy lies in modifying your thought processes. Guilt, like worry, prevents you from fully participating in the here and now. Treat the past as a learning experience. Decide that you're sorry, but what's done is done, and thinking about it further is a waste of time. That goes for the Big Regrets—your failed marriage, your aversion to studying in college, and the multifarious pangs of conscience dating back to the spelling test you cheated on in third grade.

Here's how to cut short some typical guilt trips:

I'm a terrible housekeeper. By whose standards? If yours, lower them. If by the standards of your spouse or other housemates, get them to pitch in. If the jobs can't be distributed equitably, hire a maid. Keep aware of your priorities. If sweeping the floor every day doesn't rank highly in your values scheme, it's perfectly reasonable to spend as little time on it as possible.

I'm never on time for work. Why are you late? If you dread the job, begin scouting around for a more agreeable one. If you're just groggy and slow in the morning, adjust your schedule to allow getting to bed and getting up twenty minutes earlier. You can grab a cup of coffee, miss the rush of traffic, and arrive feeling composed and competent—as well as guilt free.

I really should get more exercise. So what's stopping you? Instead of thinking about it, set this book aside right now and do twenty-five sit-ups. View this as day one of a new regimen. Then you'll also feel less guilty about the half-pan of fudge brownies you ate after dinner.

I ought to spend more time with my children. Set aside next Saturday for a family outing, letting them choose the time and destination. Preserve time during each day, perhaps the dinner hour or bedtime, to talk together on a one-to-one basis. Don't continue to worry or wonder if they're feeling neglected. Ask them. They'll probably look at you in surprise and say, "No. Now can I finish my homework?"

ANY JOB THAT'S WORTH DOING...

Perfectionism is an impractical if not impossible goal. In its pursuit, we can become so bogged down in niggling details that we lose all sense of priority and proportion. Absorbed in processes, we lose sight of objectives. For example, the perfect employee who works past quitting time retyping a dozen shipping orders instead of using correction fluid to fix her mistakes; the perfect homemaker who spends all morning polishing silverware but can go weeks without washing the floor; the perfect wife who arranges her day around errands listed by her husband; and worst, the perfect mother who supplants all her own aims and ambitions in an all-out effort to raise perfect children.

Perfection is elusive because it is so subjective. Ask yourself who is setting these sky-high standards? Who besides you is keeping score? Even if others *are* interested in your achievements, they're judging them with an entirely different set of expectations and objectives. You could devote years to designing the "perfect" computerized order-processing system for your company, but your boss won't be impressed if he needed it within three months. In most organizations, promotions don't come to the person who works the hardest, but to the person who produces results.

Beware of using perfectionism as an excuse and a delaying tactic to avoid being evaluated.

Andrea is a talented oil painter, but so far her efforts are stacked in the basement. Her friends have urged her to submit them to a local gallery or take part in the sidewalk art fair, but she declines. "Wait until I've produced a masterpiece," she has insisted for four years. As long as her work isn't for sale, it can't be rejected.

Elsie is the only woman in her circle of friends who has never hostessed a luncheon or bridge group. "My house doesn't look nice enough," she tells herself. "Maybe after we paint the living room or replace the couch."

The same arsenal of excuses ("I am just hard to please"; "I have very high standards") works for Kathie, who hasn't begun her master's thesis because she still hasn't found the right topic, and Bernice, who would make a magnificent macramé wall hanging for the hallway if she could just find the perfect color and texture of jute.

The most insidious thing about perfectionism is that it masquerades as a virtue. "If something is worth doing, it's worth doing right." "If you want a job done right, do it yourself." A more useful motto is: "It's not to do the job right but to do the right job." And do it within a reasonable time limit.

Perfection is an appropriate goal if you are a trapeze artist or brain surgeon. The rest of us should just shoot for excellence.

TOMORROW, FOR SURE...

Procrastination threads its way through each of the time-management hangups just discussed. It is an outgrowth of perfectionism and it produces guilt. Mixed with worry and indecisiveness, it can bring the most gainful endeavor to a paralyzing halt.

Procrastination is a familiar and almost universal behavioral pattern. It is inevitable, in the course of ordering our priorities, that some tasks should be delayed or neglected. Sometimes the delay works to our advantage: By putting something off until the last possible minute, we gain impetus and momentum. We may work faster and more efficiently under pressure of a deadline.

But chronic procrastination in one or more areas of your life can be destructive. There's Marsha, who has accumulated almost enough college credits for three separate degrees. Every time she gets close to graduating, she decides to change majors and puts off finding a job for another two years. JoAnne and Tom have been drifting for months in a dead-end relationship. She knows she should break it off, but dreads the confrontation. Instead she keeps hoping he'll change, or that the old spark will magically be rekindled.

> Procrastination often takes root in childhood, when it is "the most readily available and powerful means for a child to handle conflicts with parents," according to Dr. Michael Sacks, associate professor of psychiatry at New York Hospital-Cornell Medical Center. "The child is told to clean his room, and replies that he will do it, but not right now." Procrastination gives him a chance to resist parental domination and to assert autonomy and control.
>
> Later, the child may continue to use delaying tactics with other authority figures, such as teachers or bosses.[1]

The student who is always behind in homework becomes the manager who misses production deadlines. Procrastination may be related to perfectionism. ("I can't turn in the report until I am certain it contains no mistakes.") More subtly, it may be a way of avoiding responsibility. ("If I put this off long enough, maybe it will no longer have to be done. Maybe someone else will do it for me.")

The basis of procrastination is usually not laziness but fear. The root-canal work you've been postponing represents fear of pain. The

[1]Diana Benzaia, "Procrastination: Your Biggest Hang-Up," *Harper's Bazaar*, February, 1979, p. 60.

bank loan application you haven't yet mailed involves fear of rejection. The consulting business you keep saying you'll start "some day" is linked with fear of failure.

To conceal the real reasons for putting things off—often even from ourselves—we simply stay "so busy," we don't know where the day goes. Or we exclaim, in bewilderment, "I'm so swamped with things to do...." "Too busy" is the ultimate subterfuge; the skilled procrastinator stuffs her day with activities, many of them unnecessary, so that she truly has no time left to finish her doctoral thesis; schedule a medical check-up; clean the hamster's cage.

What about you? What tasks or ambitions are you not confronting? What kinds of behavior would you like to change? Don't procrastinate! Resolve that you are going to start *now* to bring all those less-than-satisfactory parts of your life under control.

Good *time* management is predicated on *self* management. Indecisiveness, anxiety, guilt, perfectionism, and procrastination can make your life an obstacle course. They can sabotage your time and your self-control. And procrastination may be the hardest of all habits to overcome. The step-by-step plan in the next chapter will help you deal with procrastination in general, as well as with any effort or undertaking you've been procrastinating about.

(4)

Taking Control

The new you is emerging: Decisive, rational, self-propelled. How can you keep on this new, positive course?

"Your goal is not just to eliminate old behaviors," Chauncey Smith says, "but to replace them with new, more desirable ones." Instead of dwelling on your past practices and the problems they caused, think positively about the new habits you're forming. Focus on your continuing improvement; your forthcoming success.

So you were a disorganized slob. You were habitually late for appointments. You had eight weeks of unanswered mail on your desk and green fuzzy growths on the leftovers in the refrigerator. That's no longer relevant. What matters is that you are ready and capable of bringing these situations under control.

From now on, don't concentrate on where you've been but where you're going.

Instead of:	Say:
"I've always been a rotten housekeeper."	"I'm going to organize my belongings so that they're easier to keep straight."
"If I lose this contract it will be disastrous."	"I will not worry about events over which I have no control."
"I'm so ashamed of those years I fought with my parents."	"I'll try from now on to improve our relationship."
"I can't resist a bargain."	"I'll stick within my budget."
"I should have finished this by now."	"I'm making slow but sure progress."
"I have never been able to...."	"From now on I will!"

Before setting out to change your behavior, Smith says, it is important to have at least neutral feelings about where you are at the moment. Accept yourself. Instead of brooding over your faults ("I'm never on time with my tax return"), dwell on your strong points ("I'm always prompt about favors I've promised to do for friends").

In short, launch your self-improvement effort as you would any other project, with a positive frame of mind. Don't generate anxiety by wishing you'd taken action sooner or worrying that you'll fail. Expect success.

The key to exchanging all your cumbersome habits and hang-ups for a smooth system of time- and self-management is behavior modification.

TAKING CHARGE

When it was first coined, the phrase "behavior modification" was sometimes linked to frontal lobotomies, psychedelic drugs, and electric shock treatments. Today, psychologists refer to it as simply a useful process for influencing behavior, stressing rewards rather than punishments. It's neither painful nor mysterious. On the contrary, you set the goals, make the rules, and reap the benefits.

The five-step plan outlined here can be adapted to any condition or problem that obstructs your self-management goals. You can use it to lose weight, quit smoking, become more assertive at work, and more responsive and relaxed at home. It provides a framework and built-in incentives for refinishing a grand piano, writing a three-act play, or saving enough money to spend a year backpacking through Europe. And here it is:

1. Define the problem, goal, or both.
2. Set a reasonable deadline.
3. Divide the goal and deadline into a series of small steps.
4. Find a model—someone who has been through what you're attempting and has achieved success.
5. Set up a reward system for progress and accomplishment.

Last September, Abby agreed to chair the PTA's annual spring carnival. Now it's March and she still hasn't assigned all the committees nor lined up concessionaires. The longer she delays, the more the pressures build. The more she dreads the work ahead, the harder it is to get started.

The problem: Abby's procrastination is a threat to the success of the carnival and to her own mental health. Blaming herself for lack of planning only makes her feel more anxious and guilty.

Solution and deadline: Take action now. Firm up within two weeks all commitments from food vendors, entertainers, and other volunteers.

Small steps: Abby drafts a letter to be circulated to all school parents, asking for help. She calls a meeting of those who volunteer, solicits suggestions, and assigns tasks. She blocks out two hours every morning for making a minimum number of phone calls until all functions are filled. Once the momentum is underway and things begin falling in place, the project seems more and more manageable.

Model: Abby had been reluctant to call on last year's carnival chairperson, believing that woman had done her share and shouldn't be bothered. Also, she was embarrassed to admit she needed help. As it turned out, the predecessor was flattered to be contacted and happy to lend advice and support.

Reward: Abby saves her morning coffee and newspaper until after she's finished her round of phone calls. But her biggest reward is the relief she is feeling from seeing the job finally being accomplished.

Sheila has been working for seven years as a librarian, but she dreams of opening her own photographic studio. She sees herself doing portraits, selling pictures to newspapers and magazines, and some day maybe even opening a gallery or publishing a book of her own work.

The problem: Sheila has a chance to buy some second-hand lab equipment at a very good price. With the equipment, she could turn her amateur picture-taking into a profitable business. The investment would pay for itself. If the venture fails, however, Sheila will be out thousands of dollars. She's afraid to take the plunge, yet afraid that such an opportunity may not present itself again.

Solution: Sheila decides to buy the equipment and, at first, to rent time on it to other photographers. She retains her library job part-time so that she'll have a steady income while she builds the second business.

Deadline: Her goal is to turn a profit from her photography within two years.

Small steps: Buying the equipment was the first step. Next, Sheila reserves space in a two-week summer photography workshop so that she can expand her technical skills. She advertises her services in the telephone yellow pages and in the classified sections of several newspapers. Still lacking a studio, she states, "I specialize in informal portraits in your own home."

Model: The photography workshop provides access to professional photographers who not only share with Sheila their ideas on photo technique, but also on business and bookkeeping skills. Sheila also gets practical advice and support by joining a women's business-owners group in her community, and the local chamber of commerce.

Reward: Working two jobs, with all her savings tied up in cameras and processing equipment, Sheila has no time or money to indulge in material rewards. So she sets time aside each day for recreational reading and a long soak in the tub. Ultimately, she knows that success in her own business will be reward in itself.

These five steps can be applied to any temporary but unproductive behavior pattern, or a major lifestyle change. Each step has its own role and importance to producing your goal. Here's a more detailed look.

DEFINING THE PROBLEM

Some people drift along for months or years feeling "vaguely discontented." They put up with an unsatisfactory job or marriage, carefully dodging the problems, hoping that they will go away. They choose to compromise, rather than confront the risky—but potentially rewarding—possibilities of change. This is living a life at half measure. The same energy being absorbed in avoiding an issue can be spent in resolving it.

"When my spirits are low, I make a mental list of what is wrong," says Nancy, a twenty-nine year-old writer and editor. "I then go through the list and decide which of these elements I can exert some control over. I channel all of my energy toward the things I can change and try not to waste time worrying about the rest.

"When something in particular bothers me more than I think it should," she continues, "I take out a piece of paper and write about it. I state what's wrong, how I feel, why I feel that way. When a problem is all down there in black and white, it's sometimes easier to evaluate, and a solution is more likely to present itself. I don't think it's ever taken me more than a page to work an issue through. I save the page in a private place for as long as it seems important. When the issue is truly resolved, the paper isn't hard to let go of."

SOLVING...ONE STEP AT A TIME

Once you've owned up to a problem and all its dire consequences, put it aside. Rivet your mind firmly on your goal. Now, instead of thinking negatively about a troublesome situation, you're thinking positively about ways to handle it and how good it will be to have the problem resolved. You can accomplish far more in an optimistic, goal-oriented frame of mind than in a mood of frustration and doubt.

A deadline gives your goal additional structure and substance. It represents an even more firm, formal promise that "not only am I going to do this, but I have decided *when* to do it and how long I expect it to take." A deadline, even though you are free to modify it later if necessary, converts good intentions into serious commitment. It also allows you to begin thinking past the deadline to those glorious days when life will be better because your goal will be fulfilled.

Find a role model. In your office, your neighborhood, your League of Women Voters chapter, or elsewhere among your acquaintances is a woman who has already been through what you're setting out to do. She started her own freelance photography business; she returned to work after having a baby; she turned twelve years of volunteer fundraising experience into a paying job; she adopted a handicapped child.

Or maybe—just as important—she has learned to do *less.* She doesn't seem to be as harassed as you feel, even though you both seem to be juggling the same multiple responsibilities and roles. Whatever it is you admire about her, ask her how she does it. Find several women who have ideas to share, and form a network.

It's no secret that programs such as Weight Watchers and Alcoholics Anonymous owe much of their success to the advice and moral support that is exchanged within the group. Whatever it is you're attempting to do, you'll save lots of time, trial, and error by finding a role model who knows the ropes and has achieved success.

The most important element of behavior modification is success. Not just trumpets and skyrockets as you achieve your ultimate goal, but a little firecracker now and then as you make visible progress. How do you insure this progress? By breaking up any overwhelming, intimidating project into a series of tiny, easily managed parts. Make the first step the smallest of all: Make a phone call; lay out the materials you'll need; block out a space of time *today* to begin.

Take your desk, which since Christmas has been spilling over with giftwrapping paper, ribbon and tape, recipe books, magazine clippings, cards and envelopes, unpaid bills, and also (you hope) the list of thank-you notes you still haven't written. Step one is getting out a large plastic trash bag. Now bring it over near the desk. See how easy this is? You can divide your work on the desk according to task (clear surface; file papers; and so forth) or by time-scheduled segments. At home in Sycamore, Illinois, Joan, a busy mother of three, prods herself to reorganize the cupboards by setting a kitchen timer for fifteen minutes. "It's such a short time, I tell myself; I can stand that. But I usually get done so much more than I expected, I begin feeling really inspired and keep right on going."

The divide-and-conquer approach makes any task unformidable; it converts mountains to molehills. To tackle the status report that has been hanging over your head at work, make some phone calls for the information you need; begin gathering data from the files; draw up an outline; write the first paragraph. Or on your long-time desire to start a career in real estate, begin studying the trends reflected in the local newspaper's classified section; take out some books from the library; make an appointment with a broker; sign up for an adult education class.

Kaye applied the "small-steps" strategy to losing weight. She'd been on and off diets for years, but inevitably became discouraged by the slow pace of her progress. "The diets all promised instant results—you know, twenty pounds in one weekend. If I couldn't match that—and I never could—I felt cheated. I would simply give up," she relates. Finally Kaye realized that while twenty pounds had remained an elusive goal, she had repeatedly been able to lose two or three pounds at one time. Cumulatively, those losses now numbered in the hundreds! So she revised her plan, making up her mind to lose one pound a week and keep it off. The progress was much slower than she would have preferred, but it was progress nonetheless. Instead of feeling despair over her consistent failure, she began to feel encouraged and elated.

IGNITING YOUR FUSE

How do you motivate yourself to do something really unpleasant? Not just lengthy or boring or messy or thankless, but all of these? Something such as: cleaning a smelly, scummy oven encrusted with grease spatters, burnt crumbs, and rock hard, baked-on cherry pie filling?

This takes a degree of self-discipline in which many of us are sorely inexperienced. We are attuned to the leisure society where the philosophies are: Take it easy; enjoy the moment; don't push yourself too hard; let someone else do the dirty work. It's hard to resist these arguments. There are so many pleasant alternatives clamoring for our attention.

But sooner or later will come the day of reckoning, when thinking about this crummy task is more depressing than doing it and getting it over with. You can wait for that ultimatum or you can skip the excuses and delay tactics and start now. Stop dreading the drudgery ahead, and think only about how good it will feel to have it finished!

Here are a few tricks to get you going:

- Ease in. Coddle yourself by resolving to do just a certain amount. Even the smallest headway gives you some momentum and makes the entire task look more manageable.
- Do the worst first. You'll be over the hump, and the rest of the job will look like a cinch by comparison.
- Set a time frame for your project and stick to it. Plan in advance to spend from 3 to 5 P.M. Saturday figuring out the income tax, and don't let anything intervene. In case of a phone call or other interruption, explain re-

gretfully but firmly that you have a previous engagement.
- Make a commitment to someone. "Promise your employer, professor, co-worker that you'll finish the report by a certain date," advises Susan, a graduate student in business administration. "You'll have to have it done by that deadline or look totally incompetent." Similarly, make a standing date for tennis to ensure that you get some regular exercise. Invite someone for dinner as an incentive to clean the house.
- Block out time when you feel thoughtful and alert. If the job requires concentration, pick a workspace where there are no distractions or interruptions. For a messy but mindless job, put on your favorite music or plan the job around a good radio talk show.
- Promise yourself a reward.

WHAT DOES IT TAKE TO MAKE YOU HAPPY?

To achieve a goal, or a least make discernible progress, is reward in itself; or, as Ralph Waldo Emerson said, "the reward of a thing well done is to have done it."

Still, a little praise doesn't hurt. Neither does an occasional trophy, an armful of roses, or a big fat cashier's check.

Look at it this way. The prospect of "getting it done and over with" may be all the incentive you need, but perhaps the promise of a good movie or dinner, a refreshing swim, or an hour of relaxed reading will spur you to work faster or better. Don't think of a reward as self-indulgent, but as a useful device to keep up your spirits and hasten your progress.

"Reinforcement comes in three categories," Chauncey Smith says. "Intellectual reinforcement can come from one's job, a challenging crossword puzzle, a theater presentation, the Sunday *New York Times;* physical reinforcement runs the gamut from food to sports activities to sex." Or, he continues, "It can come from a creative pastime like gardening or a destructive habit like smoking or drugs.

"Social reinforcement is the least tangible but often the most powerful" type of reinforcement, Smith explains. "It includes the recognition you may win from colleagues and strangers; the affection of family and friends. Most rewards are a combination of these," Smith notes. "A stimulating discussion mixes intellectual and social reinforcement; a dinner conversation integrates all three."

He recommends making up a whole menu of items and events *you* find reinforcing. Think about what you look forward to most in your daily routine:

- A midmorning coffee break
- A martini before dinner
- That peaceful hour after the baby is put to bed for a nap

Schedule your most obnoxious jobs *ahead* of those parts of the day you look forward to. Build the job into the reward system instead of the other way around.

Now expand your master reward list with all those frivolous plans or purchases you've always considered yourself too practical for:

- A thirty-minute massage
- An introductory pilot's lesson
- A quart jar of Macadamia nuts

Or think back about the things you enjoyed five years ago that you haven't done for a long time like roller skating, calling up a friend from the old neighborhood, or rereading your high-school yearbook.

Whenever you need a small thrust, reward a less preferred activity with a more preferred one. With a large inventory of preferred activities close at hand, you should never suffer from a lack of incentive.

Tools

What will it take to get you organized? A consciousness-raising seminar at Big Sur? A $300 designer briefcase? Save your money. The basic tools of organization are probably available right now in your own home or office: A pad of paper, a calendar, and a cardboard box about twelve inches square.

A "To-Do" list (the pad of paper) consolidates all the trivial but necessary chores you'd like to accomplish today—pick up clothes from the dry cleaner, send a birthday card, arrange a parent-teacher conference, take the roast out of freezer, have the oil checked. It's not the place to record multi-hour projects—you're not likely to forget them—but to note down those tasks that can be done within five to thirty minutes; (thus you don't need a reminder for "plant garden," but you do need ones for "check fertilizer supply" and "buy onion sets").

You may think it takes more time and trouble to write down such things than it does to remember them. It doesn't. Have you ever tried to compose an important, sensitive letter while the words "Buy Cat Food!" flashed on and off in your brain? Putting such thoughts on paper unclutters your mind, letting it concentrate on higher level objectives. "The important aspect of a to-do list is not what it helps you remember but what it allows you to forget," management consultant Dr. Robert T. Riley points out. "It is hard to conceive of a less meaningful use of mental energy than the remembering of things to be done."[1]

If you jot down your "things to do" on the back of an old envelope or paper napkin, you'll probably mislay it and fall even further

---

[1]Robert T. Riley, *How to Manage Your Time Successfully* (Dallas: The Drawing Board, Inc.), p. 23.

behind. Instead, use a small three-by-five-inch spiral tablet or notebook and keep it handy to jot down your ideas as soon as you think of them. Inveterate list users insist that the habit keeps them sane. They also report that it's enormously satisfying to scratch things off the list once they're accomplished.

"Ambitious, advance-minded people can always conceive of more things to do than there is possibly time for," Riley points out. "Thus, it is essential to develop a system for selecting out those items which are most urgent and/or important."[2]

Some people find it useful to set priorities with a system of ABCs, asterisks, or underlining to denote levels of importance. The lists not only provide a record of what you've done but of what kinds of tasks you keep putting off. If you find a "C"-level errand being carried over from day to day, reconsider whether it's really worth doing in the first place.

A second method of list utilization—a favorite anecdote of all time-management experts—is retold in the story of Charles Schwab. Schwab, then president of U.S. Steel, approached an efficiency expert at a meeting and said that he didn't have time to listen to him at length, but wondered if the man had any suggestions for him.

"Every morning," the expert said, "make a list of the things you have to do that day. List them in order of importance. Then concentrate on the first task until it's finished without diverting your attention to anything else. Then go on to the second one, finishing as much as you can in the course of the day." Schwab reportedly looked at the man, shrugged, and asked what he wanted for the suggestion. "Try it for a month," was the reply, "and then pay me what you think it's worth."

Thirty days later, Schwab put a check in the mail for $10,000.

A calendar-planning guide is a step more sophisticated than the basic To-Do list, but it could be just the tool to help you see precisely how you're using your time now and how to schedule in those goals that are getting sidetracked. Available in a wide range of styles and sizes, calendar planning guides come with pages sectioned off by months, weeks, days, or hours, and in models that range from simple paperbacks to deluxe editions with leather bindings and monograms. Some incorporate indexed address sections, and room for recording travel ex-

[2]Ibid. pp. 24-25.

penses, important dates, and other memoranda. Your choice will depend on whether your activities occur in fifteen-minute segments or half-day chunks; you can find the most suitable version for you at any stationery or office-supply store—or you can buy a blank notebook and customize your own.

The clear, open spaces in these booklets impel you to pen in your most worthwhile intentions and obligations. "The most important function of calendar guides," Robert Riley says, "is to drive home the concept that it's up to *you* to plan your day rather than allow others to plan it for you. Certainly other people will have some influence on your schedule, but to approach each day with a 'take me, I'm yours' attitude will simply leave you further behind and frustrated."

Start thinking in terms of *commitments* rather than *appointments,* Riley stresses.[3] Don't just use the planning guide to note activities that involve other people but also things you want to do yourself. Mark off "block time," when you can work without interruptions, and do this several days or weeks in advance so that you are first in line for your own time. Shoot for eight to sixteen hours of such time a week, he advises, using the largest blocks of time you can manage.

A large wall calendar with plenty of space around each date for noting birthdays, appointments, school holidays, and other events is the control center of your household. The key to making it work is to insist that each family member old enough to read and write make a point of consulting and contributing to it. Some large families color-code the agenda for each individual—Becky's soccer practice and babysitting job is recorded in red, Dad's out-of-town meeting is noted in green, and so on.

At the beginning of the year, take the calendar and mark down all of your relatives' birthdays and anniversaries, school vacation dates, the dates of home football games, and any other events of standing importance. Make each person in the household responsible for recording upcoming events as soon as they're definite—not only as personal reminders but also to prevent others from making conflicting plans. A community calendar is particularly crucial in a household with teenagers, for reference in planning meals, coordinating use of the car(s), and ferreting out time together.

[3]Ibid., p. 25.

A blackboard, bulletin board, or set of refrigerator magnets is essential for conveying up-to-the-minute messages or reminders. Most likely the problem is not that you lack these devices, but that you own all three. Designate *one* place in the house for members to check for messages to one another when they leave and come home.

A household filing system can be improvised from a box about twelve inches square that can accommodate a dozen or more letter-sized file folders. If you have a home business or lots of hobbies, or simply tend to be a pack rat, you may find that an authentic two- or three-drawer office-model filing cabinet is a worthy investment. But a sturdy cardboard box will get you started.

Your household files serve two main functions. In financial matters, they make certain records easily accessible (such as at income-tax time) and help you to see how much money is coming and going so that you can budget ahead; and they provide compact, orderly storage for information you wish to keep on anything of interest.

In organizing the filing system in your home, as in the office (see Chapter 7), think in terms of a few broad categories, not dozens of subheadings. For example, you don't need separate pockets for your automobile registration, insurance, repair receipts, and waxing instructions. One folder marked "car" is sufficient.

The exception is "bills and receipts." If—like most people—you acquire these in great quantities, you'll find it practical to separate them by month or by type, such as "utilities" or "medical expenses." Here are the divisions that work for me:

Monthly expenses: Contains the customer-receipt portion of credit-card statements, charge accounts, installment loans, utilities, and miscellaneous expenses such as the piano tuner or your child's summer camp fee. Also, use this section to keep receipts from the day-care center or your babysitter—they're tax deductible. Mark the date and the amount paid on the portion of the bill you keep.

Income: Pay-check stubs, savings account passbooks, savings certificates, and records of investment, such as stocks, bonds, or real estate.

Checking account: Your monthly statements, after you've reconciled them, and cancelled checks. Once a year, sort out the checks that can be used for tax deductions.

Income tax: Records of business expenses, finance charges, charitable contributions, and medical bills. If these are filed within a different folder, such as "credit cards" or "health care," make a note here so that they can be easily retrieved for April 15. Keep copies of tax returns for the past three years; earlier returns may be relegated to the "inactive" files box in the garage or attic.

House: Copy of mortgage, payment statements, insurance, and receipts for any home improvements such as insulation, landscaping, or major repairs.

Car: Service records, repairs, insurance, copy of registration, and maintenance information.

Appliances: Sales receipts, warranties, and operating instructions.

Personal papers: Copies of family birth certificates, marriage certificates, wills, discharge and service records, and divorce and property settlement agreements. Originals of these should be kept in a safe-deposit box.

Refundables: Sales slips, price tags, guarantees, and mail order receipts. As merchandise becomes progressively more expensive but not necessarily more reliable, you should routinely keep these items in case you need to make an exchange or demand a refund.

The remaining space may be used for any kinds of files that suit your personal interests. If you entertain often, keep a folder of favorite menus and recipes, or wine suggestions; or keep one of restaurant reviews. For your kids, keep a folder for each, with his or her report cards, exceptional essays, and artwork. For your volunteer activities, keep separate folders for the Scouts, the city planning committee, or the League of Women Voters. For your hobbies, keep folders containing newspaper or magazine clippings on decorating ideas, craft designs, and gardening tips.

A household "tickler file" can be inserted in your regular file box or can be kept in a separate location. This device, with twelve monthly pockets, helps you keep track of future events. Store, in the appropriate slot, theater tickets, reminder cards for the car's tune-up, birthday cards, and gift suggestions—or any variety of ideas for future follow-up.

Finally, designate one folder, basket, or other container with the heading "to be filed" for items in process. Make sure it is not too large, so that you won't be tempted to let the contents get out of control.

6

The Chances
of a
Lifetime

Life is either a daring adventure or nothing.
Helen Keller

Exactly what do you want out of life? Have you thought about it lately?

I don't mean twenty years from now—the world is changing too fast for such remote speculation. But where are you hoping to be six months or six weeks from now? What will you accomplish today?

As already described, the five-step behavioral-change plan outlined in Chapter 4 has numerous applications. It can help you:

- Demolish bad habits, such as procrastination, tardiness, or smoking.
- Finally accomplish big unpleasant tasks you've been procrastinating about, like hanging the storm windows or cleaning out the garage.
- Spur you on toward the *positive* goals of your life, such as owning your own business, hooking a nine-by-twelve-foot rug, or mastering conversational French.

45

The positive goals are the most gratifying—provided you know what they are. If your personal crystal ball is malfunctioning, it could be that you're telling yourself:

I'm just overwhelmed. There are so many things to do and be and try that I don't know where to begin. I feel like a kid in a candy store. I'll just keep browsing instead of committing myself.

Some day my prince will come. He'll take me away from all of this. I'll follow *his* destiny. I'll just bide my time meanwhile.

Spontaneity is everything. Life shouldn't be planned. It should just "happen." I'll just sit here quietly and pay attention in case something should happen to me.

What if I fail? Planning is risky. If I admit what I really want out of life, I just set myself up for a disappointment.

Who has time to make plans? I just bounce from crisis to crisis.

That last excuse is probably the most familiar. It's easy to get so caught up in routine activities that we lose sight of how much time they are taking and why we got involved in them in the first place. To illustrate:

Gail awakens at 7 A.M. feeling peppy and full of purpose. Today she will get lots accomplished. She rouses Steve and Martha, ages eleven and eight, fixes their breakfast, and helps them hunt for their homework. By 8:45 they are running late, so she drives them the five blocks to school.

Back home she contemplates starting on the homework assignment due for this evening's accounting class. The calculator is missing. She goes to look for it in the children's playroom, which resembles the aftermath of the Great Earthquake. Almost automatically she begins to make piles of the books, toys, and clothing. Reconsidering, she gathers up the littered clothes and starts to do a load of laundry. Her neighbor Lyn calls to ask if she can come over and borrow a set of screwdrivers, and Gail decides she'd better make the kitchen look more presentable. She puts on a pot of coffee and Lyn stays and chats until the kids come home for lunch. They know where the calculator is; but the batteries are dead.

In the afternoon, Gail arrives at the architectural firm where she works as a part-time bookkeeper. She is about to tackle a pile of invoices when her boss asks her to sit in on a meeting for him and take notes. When she gets back to her desk, Liz the receptionist is waiting to relate episode ninety-four of her marital problems. Gail leaves the office late, taking an armload of invoices to finish at home. School is out. Her children are perched indignantly on the doorstep.

Gail decides to placate them by baking some oatmeal cookies. But before the cookies are out of the oven, Steve is out the door, yelling that he'll be at a friend's house. Martha wails frantically that there is a hole in her leotard just as the carpool to her ballet class pulls into the driveway. Gail quickly sews up her daughter's leotard, apologizes to the driver, and rushes back to the kitchen to retrieve the pan full of cookies, burnt to cinders.

Nothing is defrosted for dinner, so Gail begins stirring up a tuna casserole. Midway through the recipe, she discovers that what she thought was a can of tuna fish is actually cat food. She hustles off to the supermarket just as it swells with hordes of after-work shoppers. Only after she arrives back home with her solitary purchase does she remember that she still has no batteries for the calculator; it doesn't matter, she has neither the time nor the energy to finish the homework assignment.

Days like this vividly illustrate how "time gets away from us" if it is not firmly anchored by plans and goals. How about you? Do you see yourself moving toward certain concrete objectives? Or are you just puttering about, keeping the house picked up, the boss satisfied, the family fed, and yourself out of trouble? It takes a conscious, persistent effort to transform wishful thinking into a dream come true. It begins with putting into words exactly what you expect of yourself.

Time-management experts use a number of tricks to start people thinking in terms of objectives and goals:

First: Picture a perfect day for yourself three years from now. Where will you be? On the deck of a cruise ship? On a podium before the members of Congress? How will you look? Twenty pounds thinner? Nine months pregnant? What will you be doing? How will you feel? Inevitably the question arises, What are you doing *now* to make this scenario become a reality?

Second: Picture yourself at the age of seventy-five, looking back on your most satisfying experiences and accomplishments. What kinds of things would constitute—for you—a full life? Making a contribution to your field, perhaps by publishing a musical composition or defining a new theory in nuclear physics? Or would you find more contentment in the memory of close friendships, service to your community, and spiritual growth? In other words, understand your values, and then consider whether your current activities are compatible with them or in conflict.

Third: Take a pencil and paper and write as many endings as possible to the sentence, "One of the things I'd really like to do during my life is...." Include every thought that comes to mind, from the practical to the fantastic. Take a few days to compile this list. Then separate the items into the following categories: **(A)** of prime importance and fully within your capabilities; **(B)** worthwhile but of secondary priority; and **(C)** probably unrealistic. Set the B and C lists aside, where they won't be distracting, and get busy on the A list today.

Time-management expert Alan Lakein recommends making lists for immediate and long-range goals, and ranking the top three priorities in each A-1, A-2, and A-3. In *all* planning, he says, make a list and set priorities. Any time you find yourself drifting or spinning your wheels, ask Lakein's Question: "What is the best use of my time right now?"[1]

Review your major goals on a regular basis, perhaps on your birthday or on New Year's Eve. Go through your daily objectives at the beginning of each day, as you're showering or driving to work. And take stock of your situation whenever you feel you're at a "turning point," whether it's graduation from college, your wedding day, or the infamous "mid-life crisis."

Be specific in contemplating your goals. Avoid hazy concepts such as "to be happy" or "well liked" or "achieving financial security." Does financial security mean a Swiss bank account or twenty dollars tucked under the mattress?

How do you know which of your goals are realistic? Consider your circumstances. One of your most persistent ambitions may be to restore a Victorian townhouse, but it can't be ranked as an "A" goal if the mortgage rates just jumped to 16 percent and you're due for a transfer to Houston. Your goals must inevitably be evaluated in the context of your environment, and limited to those aspects that are within your control.

And look at your assets. Not just your financial assets—although they certainly count—but your personality, experience, and inborn talents. Tally up your strengths and weaknesses and decide whether they enhance or hinder your chances at a particular goal.

[1]Alan Lakein, *How to Get Control of Your Time and Your Life* (New York: Peter H. Wyden, Inc., 1973), pp. 28, 96.

Ever since she was a teenager, Laura has wanted to be an investigative reporter in Washington. On the plus side she ranks a Master's degree from the Columbia School of Journalism, three years of reporting on a medium-sized daily, and a strong interest in public affairs. She is curious, energetic, and in good health.

On the minus side, Laura values financial security. Several months of job hunting in Washington will wipe out her savings, probably even put her in debt. She has strong ties to her family and has never lived more than an hour's commute from her parents. She has a tendency to appear shy and unassertive, a disadvantage in finding a competitive job and dealing with politicians. On the other hand, she concludes finally, she is motivated and ambitious enough to overcome the handicaps.

I believe in taking risks, whatever the odds. Even the failures—perhaps especially the failures—help us sort out exactly where our values lie, where we should invest our personal resources. The more goals we set for ourselves, the better. With plenty of irons in the fire, a failure here and there along the way will not seem so tragic. Just as time management helps us achieve goals, goal-seeking improves time-management skills.

Laura, for example, may become a Pulitzer Prize-winning writer for the *Washington Post*. Or she may become fed up with the superficial aspects of the Capital scene and head back to the Cornbelt. She may decide to abandon journalism altogether and open a boutique in Georgetown. *Any* of these outcomes is better than staying in Iowa for five more years and speculating about how her life would have been different.

7

Office Hours

"When I was out of a job, I thought, hey, this isn't so bad. I can live off my savings and unemployment, catch up on my reading, repaint the apartment," says Cynthia, a twenty-nine-year-old financial analyst. "When the right thing comes along, I'll take it, but meanwhile I can use the time to catch up on all the things I've been really wanting to do.

"It didn't work out like I planned. By the third week I could hardly drag myself out of bed in the morning. I was depressed and listless. Trivial things took up all my time. I never realized how much of my self-image and daily routine had depended on my job. I didn't snap out of my stupor until—you guessed it—I started working again."

"What do you want to be when you grow up?" the adult asks the child. "What's your major?" asks the college student. "And what do you *do*?" asks the cocktail party guest. A large part of our identity is bound up with what we do for a living.

A generation ago, women weren't asked. Or the question was altered somewhat. ("What does your husband do?") Indeed, a woman thought twice before taking a job outside the home. If she was single, did it mean she despaired of getting married? If married, would she give the impression that her husband couldn't make enough money to support the family? And if she had children, well, it was common knowledge that the children of working mothers were likely to grow up feeling rejected and abandoned. They would probably wind up with jail records for stealing hubcaps.

Yet even in 1950, 34 percent of the nation's women were in the labor force, and the figure climbed steadily, topping 50 percent by the late

1970s. Within the decade 1980-1990, the U.S. Labor Department has predicted an increase from the 42 million women employed in 1980 to 54.3 million by 1990. Public opinion has changed too. In 1981, a study entitled "Today's American Women: How the Public Sees Her," prepared for the President's Advisory Committee for Women by the Public Agenda Foundation, reported unqualified acceptance by the general public of working women and their entitlement to the same jobs, pay, and responsibility levels as those of men.

While a wide gap remains between males and females in occupational pay and status, the trends are clear: More women are getting advanced degrees, entering nontraditional fields, starting their own businesses, and breaking into the executive ranks of the Fortune 500.

MORE THAN A PAYCHECK

Identity, income, and independence. A job promises all of these things, but it doesn't fulfill them. You, the employee, achieve them by doing the job right.

The satisfactions of being hired or promoted fade quickly if you find you've accepted a responsibility and aren't handling it. You fail to meet your sales quota two months in a row; you haven't begun the report that was due last Friday; you habitually slink into meetings (as all heads turn) ten minutes late. These small errors aren't likely to get you fired, but they certainly won't earn you any commendations.

Perhaps you've been able to be quite discreet about your shortcomings. Your boss and co-workers don't even seem to suspect, but *you* know that you're not measuring up to your full potential, and that's frustrating. All of Washington's statistics on the women's employment boom are of little comfort if your own career is in a recession.

Take a moment to appraise your job and your feelings about it. What does it do for you, besides preventing overdrafts in your checkbook? Ask yourself:

- Have your responsibilities increased since the day you were hired?
- What about your salary and status?
- Are you receiving direction and instructive feedback from your superiors, adequate support from your staff, or both?

- Do you rarely feel tense, anxious, and under pressure? Or maybe just bored?
- Do you like the people the job puts you in contact with?
- Is the job fun?

If the answer is "no" to many of these questions, your problems in getting things done may not be due to lack of time but to lack of motivation. If your job doesn't offer you a challenge, a learning experience, a degree of financial security or, at the very least, a good time, you should postpone reading this chapter until you've found another one.

On the other hand, if you are happy in your job and have all the resources you need to handle it—except enough time—the strategies outlined in these pages should help.

Let's say you've found your niche, at least for the present, and you're determined to make the most of it. Even a lower rung on the career ladder needs upkeep and maintenance. Who knows where it will lead?

No matter how you feel about the job as a whole, there are probably parts of it you loathe and parts you enjoy so much you would gladly do them for free. Your goal is to organize the day so that you can finish the disagreeable tasks quickly and devote maximum time—guilt free—to the things you find more rewarding.

How you manage your time at work depends on the type of job you have. A riveter on an assembly line or a nursery school teacher has less control over her schedule than a bookkeeper or a stockbroker. This chapter focuses on the office setting, but the information can be applied to many kinds of work situations.

Think of the workday as a self-contained unit within the total day, a sphere within a sphere. Whether it's four, eight, or twelve hours long, the workday has its own agenda and timetable, its own priorities and goals. It generally has its own separate environment, unless you work in your home. And it is pervaded with distractions and interruptions, only some of which are within your control.

The first rule for increasing your competence at work is to concentrate only on problems and tasks that are job-related. The office is no place for updating a shopping list, scheduling dental appointments, or fretting about the chicken you forgot to defrost for dinner. As your thoughts drift to home or family concerns—as they inevitably will at times—add them to your To Do list. Then put the list out of sight until lunch or quitting time.

Second, create specific, realistic objectives for yourself that can be accomplished:

Within the next couple of hours
By the end of the day
By the end of the week

Write them down. You're apt to take them more seriously if you commit them to paper.

Some people balk at the concept of planning their day. They see it as a complex, tedious undertaking. Nonsense. Obviously you won't spend half the morning meticulously charting how you will spend the rest of it. *Planning* simply means thinking about your time in a systematic way. Invest your time where it counts. And finally, consider what energy level various tasks will require and what goals will be accomplished.

Nathaniel Stewart, a management consultant and director of the Institute for Women in Management, stresses the importance of thinking not in terms of how much but of how well; for what value; toward what end.

He recommends classifying your day's agenda into: (1) things that *must* be done, and why; (2) things you *want* to get done within a certain time period; (3) things that would be nice to do eventually; and (4) things that don't really need or deserve your attention.[1]

To determine where a task ranks in importance, consider whether it really contributes to some major objective—either the company's or your own. Will it aid you in making some upcoming decision, or ward off a potential problem? *Is it the best possible use of your time at this moment*? The questions must be asked repeatedly each time a new situation presents itself; each person's priorities are different.

Jan, twenty-eight, does statistical analyses for an opinion-research firm. Her most productive hours are spent hunched over a desk piled with graph sheets and computer printouts. Absorbed in some interesting findings, she will lock her door and let the telephone ring in or-

[1]Nathaniel Stewart, *The Effective Woman Manager* (New York: Wiley-Interscience, 1977), p. 162.

der to preserve her level of concentration. She rarely socializes except on evenings and weekends.

Carol, thirty-five, puts a premium on her social contacts. As a sales representative for an electronics manufacturing firm, she spends most of her week meeting with clients, demonstrating equipment, and conducting sales meetings. Telephone calls, which Jan views as a nuisance, enabled Carol to nail down nearly $40,000 in commissions last year.

Without a clear set of objectives and a plan for achieving them, you can only puddle-jump from one task to another, leaving lots of things half finished. Perhaps you've made some progress, but you *lose* ground every time you have to reorient yourself to a project and figure out where you left off. Make a habit of completing one task before you move on to another.

At the same time, don't get bogged down in detail. Sometimes—especially if you really enjoy what you're doing—it's easy to become so absorbed in a single and possibly inconsequential part of an activity that you lose sight of its place in the overall scheme of things. Solution: When you set an objective, give yourself a time frame and a deadline for completing it.

In a given situation, 20 percent of the total effort expended will produce 80 percent of the results. That observation is credited to Vilfredo Pareto, a nineteenth-century Italian sociologist and economist. The "Pareto Principle" means that:

- In a typical company, 20 percent of the products will produce 80 percent of the revenue.
- In a meeting, 20 percent of the discussion will generate 80 percent of the solutions.
- Within your workday, 20 percent of your efforts will produce 80 percent of the results.

Therefore, don't approach your job as if every aspect of it were equally important. Be deliberate about what you decide to do, when to do it, and how much effort you bestow on it. You're not a short-order cook, handling tasks one-by-one in order of appearance. You can shuffle things around to your advantage, doing urgent, important, or difficult tasks during your high-energy "prime time" and leaving routine busywork for times when it's harder to concentrate.

Don't be rigid about following the schedule, but treat it seriously. If you find yourself spending too much time on certain areas of your job, look for the reasons. Are you getting the right information and support? Can you set aside blocks of time and avert interruptions? When you get behind in a project, do you tend to try to make up for this by doing the work "perfectly," and thus finishing it even later?

Take one aspect of your job that seems to persistently take longer than it should—your weekly status report, for example—and give it a realistic time limit. Reward yourself, perhaps with a cup of coffee or a brief reading break, when you meet your deadline. If you've been putting off starting some big project, which now looms larger and more ominous because the pressure is building, break it into a series of small milestones and get it underway!

Good time-management at work mainly involves a secure understanding of the job—its objectives, priorities, and pitfalls; and yourself—your capabilities, energy levels, weaknesses, and strengths. Once you've mastered these areas, your productivity will skyrocket!

CLEAR THE DECKS

The workspace, because it's inanimate, is your most controllable asset. Organizing an office is a cinch compared with organizing a home. You have basically one desk to contend with instead of an entire house or apartment. It is one of the most functional pieces of furniture made, designed for order and accomplishment. Yet many of us render it useless by heaping it with all manner of papers, manuals, folders, unanswered mail, and other unfinished business.

"A Clean Desk Is a Sign of an Empty Mind." Now there was a slogan I could relate to! It not only excused my messy desk, it extolled it! I liked this phrase so much that I even stitched it in needlepoint.

Another rendition, however, equates a cluttered desk with a cluttered mind. It's not as catchy as the first version, but it does have a ring of truth. Reluctantly, I'm forced to admit that I have spent years trying to attach virtue to disorganization, and have decided that there is no relationship. Either you spend time putting things where they belong or you spend more time later trying to find them.

"For some business people, a stack of papers on the desk represents a sort of security blanket," notes Barbara Stahl, who leads a "Management of Managers" seminar at the University of Michigan. "The pile seems to say 'look how busy and important I am. What would they do without me!'"

True, a desk is bound to show some signs of activity, but the activity should be directed toward one thing at a time.

Most of your desk should be clear of everything except the papers you're currently dealing with. Put memos, reports, and other incoming correspondence off to one side, in your choice of an "In" container; items you've handled can go in an "Out" container to be filed or forwarded. If you're right-handed, put telephone directories and other reference books to your right; put the phone within reach of your left hand so that your writing hand is free to make notes while you're talking.

Photographs of your family, potted plants, and other paraphernalia are distracting and have no place on the work surface, insist time-management experts. Precisely because they give your desk a warm, homey appearance, they make you look less professional. Put them on a bookshelf instead.

How you organize the rest of your space, such as drawers, shelves, and filing cabinets, depends on the nature of your job and your position. But the rule of thumb is: Simplify. Save fewer things, in a smaller space, for shorter periods of time. Too many files, like the volumes of paper they contain, are a sign of insecurity. You should be familiar enough with your work to know whether any piece of material will be needed for future reference.

Finally, for those many papers that fall somewhere between the categories of "urgent" and "useless," there is that invaluable desk accessory, the Bottom Drawer. Here go all the items that aren't momentous enough to file for future generations, yet might be needed for reference during the next few weeks. It's a place for throwaways that are being kept in a "holding" pattern. Whenever the drawer gets stuffed to capacity, remove the bottom third of the pile and give it one last glance before shoving it in the wastebasket.

Paperwork probably has one of the lowest yield-for-time-spent ratios on the work docket. Your desk—the one you're supposed to keep clear for current projects—is a landing strip for the multifarious reports, requests, messages, memos, and mail being circulated by your colleagues. How tempting they look, even the reminder about new parking regulations, when you're in the middle of something boring and unpleasant. And how worrisome they can be, like that complaint letter or the four-page questionnaire you still haven't answered.

A cardinal rule of time management is: Never handle any piece of paper more than twice. Give yourself one chance to read it and one to take action on it. The sooner you take action, the better, so that you don't have to reread and reevaluate.

If your desk is currently sagging under an avalanche of memos, queries, and reports in progress, here's how to clear the decks:

1. Around midafternoon, or whenever you experience your energy slump (because the task that follows doesn't require prime concentration), gather all the papers on your desk into one stack.
2. Now sort them, a page at a time, into high-priority, low-priority, and reading material. Be very selective with that last category. If an article looks only moderately interesting and you've been meaning to read it for six months now, direct it to pile four, the wastebasket.
3. Now take the high-priority pile and arrange the papers in order of urgency, importance, or both. Put the top item in the middle of your clean desk. Having had this little break of busywork, you should be ready to sit down and take action on it.

Here are some more ways you can speed your own processing of paperwork:

- Handle it all at once. Resist the temptation to read every flyer as it lands on your desk, especially if this means breaking your prime-time concentration. Set it aside in your "In" basket until later.
- For informal correspondence, put a brief, handwritten reply on the letter and return it to the sender. This is fast and personal, and saves you from reiterating the content of the letter you're answering.
- Develop form letters for correspondence that requires a typewritten response.
- Barbara Stahl suggests the following cure for paper shufflers: "Each time you pick up a piece of paper and move it to a new spot on your desk, put a red dot on it. If you're stuck with a batch of speckled pages, you know you've got to be more decisive in your paperwork."

- Take a speed-reading course. A good self-training guide is *How to Read Better and Faster* by Norman Lewis.[2]

A secretary or assistant can save lots of time for her boss by opening and sorting incoming mail; handling routine inquiries; writing a marginal note on long letters that summarizes their key points, and discarding advertising and junk mail that are of no interest.

A final way to reduce the paper around your office is: Don't contribute to it. Be very selective about what you copy, circulate, and file for future reference. When you do decide to circulate some reading matter, take time to underline key points and paragraphs in it before attaching the routing slip.

THE TYRANNICAL TELEPHONE

Most people don't work in a vacuum. And those of us who have tried (freelance writers are an obvious example) know that prolonged isolation can be lonely and boring. So we cluster in offices humming with people, events, and things that breed constant distraction. While distractions can't be eliminated, they can certainly be reduced and controlled.

Telephones are an enormous convenience, provided, of course, that we're doing the dialing. Incoming calls are rarely convenient. They wreck our concentration, break our momentum, thwart our progress.

To make the best use of your day, it's essential to block off two or three hours of "prime time" in which to concentrate on important projects. Try to have the switchboard operator or your secretary intercept calls for you during this period, perhaps suggesting a "call back time" between 11 A.M. and noon. Or your secretary may be able to set the tone for a brief and expeditious call by offering to "see if she [you] can be interrupted."

If you work alone, consider hiring an answering service or installing a telephone answering machine to reduce interruptions.

But what if you *are* a secretary or are in a similar position that requires being constantly accessible? You can still reduce your time on the

[2]Norman Lewis, *How to Read Better and Faster* (New York: Thomas Y. Crowell, 1978).

phone by getting promptly down to business. Avoid openings like "How are you?" and "What's new?" A pleasant "What can I do for you?" steers the caller directly to the point.

When making calls, you can save time for the person on the other end by practicing the same courtesy. Announce immediately who you are and why you called. It may be a matter that the secretary can help you with. If the call will take more than two minutes, ask if you've picked a bad time and offer to call back at a time that is mutually convenient.

To further minimize the disruption, do all your phoning at one time. As with clearing the "In" box, I find telephone calls perfectly suited to the low-energy time of my day. If I make all of my calls around 11:30 A. M., I can catch most people in. And they're not apt to talk long, since they may be getting ready to go to lunch.

Are you put off by an answering machine? I used to be, but I've discovered that people who use them tend to be the most conscientious about returning calls. To assist them, be sure to leave a complete message: Your name, number, reason for calling, and when they can reach you.

For some of us, the biggest problem isn't the phone call itself but how to end it. We were brought up to be sociable and accommodating, and when someone on the other end says, "Oh, and by the way...," we sigh inwardly and listen on.

You can and must break this tendency. No one will be offended if you say:

"I'm expecting another call, so I'd better go now."

"I know you're busy so don't let me keep you."

"Someone is waiting here to see me. I'll talk to you later."

These remarks work equally well at home, where we are even more vulnerable to the social chatterbox. Here you can add one more very plausible standby: "I have to take something out of the oven."

"HI! GOT A MINUTE?"

Visitors can present more of a problem than telephone calls. Since business associates tend to make appointments, the main offenders are likely to be our friends. Fred the sales manager, for example, poised beside your desk at 9 A.M., holding a cup of coffee and chortling, "Wait until you hear what I did this weekend!"

How do you discourage Fred without alienating him? How do you at least coax the big news out of him quickly now that he's whetted your curiosity?

Use body language. Lean forward, not back, in your chair. Keep a pencil poised in your hand. Or stand while he is talking. Whatever you do, don't suggest that he be seated.

Think of something you need in the vicinity of Fred's office and begin slowly walking him back there while he is talking. Or tell him you must make a phone call but you'll drop in and see him afterward. Either way, in his office, *you* control the exit.

Your secretary can be a partner and protector against visitor interruptions. By preplanned agreement, she can step in and remind you of an upcoming obligation. That gives you an opening for bringing the conversation to a close. You can also establish regular "drop-in" hours and inform your staff and associates.

If you have a door, close it.

If you work in a cubicle or out in the open, try to arrange your desk so that you're not facing the flow of traffic (because if you think about it, once you establish eye contact, a verbal exchange is inevitable).

One administrator discourages uninvited visitors by removing the extra chairs from her office and lowering the thermostat to sixty degrees. A resourceful secretary hands her talkative friends a stack of envelopes to lick. "They either get the hint that I'm busy," she observes, "or I get some welcome assistance!"

More effective than all this chicanery, however, is to simply tell the person that he or she has come at a bad time. "I'm anxious to talk with you," you explain honestly, "but I must finish this work first. When can we get together later?" Your co-workers will appreciate your candor and will be encouraged to be just as straightforward with you when you interrupt them.

ONE MEETING AFTER ANOTHER

Meetings can be valuable time-savers for group decision-making, problem-solving, and improving communication generally. But unless thoughtfully planned and controlled, they can waste vast amounts of time for all parties involved. If you are calling the meeting:

1. Plan carefully what must be discussed and accomplished. Never hold a meeting without a purpose, or to review some matter on which you could act independently.
2. Limit the participants to those whose input is really needed. If you're planning a lengthy session, schedule each presenter for a specific time slot so that you don't tie up his or her time for longer than necessary.
3. Let each participant know the reasons for the meeting so that they will come prepared to contribute.
4. Set a time limit, and start and end on schedule. Don't hold up those who were prompt for the benefit of a few stragglers.
5. Follow a prepared agenda. If there are several items on the docket, limit the discussion on each. Call for a consensus so that you can move ahead.
6. Use a blackboard or flip chart in a large meeting to summarize points as they are made and to keep the discussion tightly focused.
7. If you reach a complete stalemate on some issue, assign one or two reliable people to gather additional data and bring a recommendation to the next meeting; but do this as a last resort. Meetings have a tendency to breed and multiply, spawning all sorts of in-house studies, committees, and task forces. You should aim to eliminate these time-gobblers, not initiate them.
8. Summarize to the group, before it disbands, what you feel has been accomplished. Reiterate any decisions or assignments.
9. If minutes are distributed, make sure they are typed and sent—both to the participants and other concerned parties—within forty-eight hours of the meeting. In most meetings, the minutes need only be a summary of actions taken—not the debate that preceded them. The last thing a meeting should do is generate more paperwork.

Some people schedule meetings an hour before lunch or quitting time, to dissuade the participants from pursuing irrelevant discussion. Others prefer to meet first thing in the morning so that they are not distracted all day by anticipating the meeting. Whatever your method, establish a reputation for holding meetings that are brief and productive. If you start on time, people will arrive on time; if you don't bring up matters that aren't on the agenda, they won't be inclined to either.

As a meeting participant, you can also do your share to keep things running smoothly. Arrive on time and prepared. Keep a separate folder for X organization and Y task force so that you have all the information you need for each group, consolidated and ready to take with you.

If you can't make a meeting or send a substitute, notify the chairperson. If some important issue will be discussed (and if not, why hold the meeting?) you can offer your views on it.

Finally, what if the organization and the issues concern you but the chairperson keeps letting the discussion get sidetracked? Raise a question related to the original issue, thus tactfully shifting the meeting back on course. Volunteer to track down some piece of information that may settle an argument. Pay attention, take notes, and as soon as you get an opening, ask "Are we ready to bring this to a vote?" Don't hesitate to assert yourself! After all, if you hadn't been expected to contribute to the meeting, you wouldn't have been invited!

The business lunch seems like such an efficient way to hold a meeting. You had to eat anyway, right? Now you're killing two birds with one stone!

But consider all the time you waste traveling to the restaurant, waiting to be seated, and —quite often—eating a heavier meal than you intended or needed.

"A typical business lunch takes up to two hours," estimates Joan, a real-estate broker. "Maybe twenty minutes of that is related to properties and financial arrangements. "This is fine," she explains, "if your aim is to establish a better social rapport. But if you strictly want to expedite some business, you'll do it much faster in an office after lunching alone on a container of yogurt."

WORKAHOLICS, ATTENTION

Breaks are the last thing you should sacrifice in order to gain time. It may seem as if working nonstop through the noon hour and into the evening is the only way to meet your deadline, but take a hard look at progress.

Sitting all day at a typewriter or drafting table is as exhausting as running a marathon, and prolonged concentration muddles even the sharpest mind. Get up and stretch. Take a walk outdoors. Run an errand. Pick up a copy of the newspaper and read something diverting, like the movie reviews. You'll work faster, more accurately, and more enthusiastically after these reviving rewards.

Delegating is a skill worth cultivating. Most women need extra practice, having been trained by parents and then husbands to be champion delegatees. It's very nice to do everything by yourself, but why should you if you have access to an able-minded secretary, assistant, or subordinate?

Managers who resist delegating are usually afraid of being disliked, of relinquishing control, or of having to take the blame, potentially, for someone else's mistakes. The perfectionist feels noble for "doing it all alone because no one else can be trusted." But she actually does others a disservice by refusing to recognize their talents. She is failing in one of her key roles as manager—developing the capabilities of others.

"No" is as hard for some women to say as "help." Agreeably, sometimes unquestioningly, you add one more short-term responsibility, one more committee membership, and one more rush assignment. You don't know that you're overextended until you are, and then it's too late. Whatever happened to *your* priorities? They have long been buried beneath everyone else's.

In the meantime, you're likely to do a half-hearted, slipshod job on these tasks that you have little interest in or time for. How does it look when you join a group and then miss half of its meetings? When you agree to coordinate a charity drive and are late in filing reports?

People often won't say "No," so as to avoid offending the person who asked their help. But how many more people will be offended if you say "Yes" and then don't follow through?

Be realistic about how much you can do—and do well. It's the one area in which you have no one else to answer to but yourself.

8

Networking

"The reason women have been slow to get ahead in business," one of my male colleagues asserts authoritatively, "is that they don't help one another. Women don't like to work for other women. If one does capture a prestigious executive post, she feels threatened by the advancement of other bright, capable females. Why? Because they represent proof that she herself is not extraordinary.

"Men are different," he goes on. "They welcome the chance to play mentor to talented subordinates. The female executive doesn't feel she owes any favors. She figures, 'I made it here without anyone's help. Other women can too.'"

What an indictment! He is describing a phenomenon that psychologists call "the Queen Bee Syndrome." It may exist, but among working women I've known it is hardly pervasive; for one reason— there haven't been that many high-ranking women executives to qualify for the role.

A different, much more positive trend is underway in the eighties. Across cities and within companies, women are banding together and serving as resources for one another. Through formal organizations and informal contacts we are sharing information, gaining advice, and getting ahead.

"Networking" has become a buzzword for the alliances forming in hundreds of new professional women's organizations that are springing up all over the country. These associations range from tightly structured invitational groups with regular meetings, elected officers, and by-laws, to large open organizations like All the Good Old Girls in Minneapolis, with only a steering committee to coordinate some 2,000 members.

65

Networking is also a function of hundreds of women's organizations that have been around for decades. The American Association of University Women is a network; so is Black Women Entrepreneurs, Inc., and the League of Women Voters. Women have long used their contacts in such organizations to get information, solve problems, and advance personal goals.

But what distinguishes the "new girl networks" from traditional organizations are the goals that are absent. In most cases you'll find no community service projects, no fundraising events. What the group *might* sponsor are monthly program meetings with speakers, or a career development workshop, where members can meet one another. Some organizations are formed to advance a cause; networks are formed to advance the membership.

Although networks foster supportive relationships, they are not a mutual aid society. Writer Jane Wilson points out that:

> The first requirement for network membership is more or less naked self-interest—and this for many women, despite the arrival of the "Me Generation," is something new. Self-esteem is a pre-requisite. To make use of others you need to feel usable yourself.
>
> In a mutual use network, everyone is expected to deal from a position of strength, actively contributing whatever information or expertise she may have. Passive members simply fail to become functioning links of the network.[1]

The exclusivity to some networks—those that only open their ranks to women who have reached a certain level of power and status—inevitably raises charges of elitism. Yet the "come one, come all" approach may create difficulties in reaching a consensus on direction and purpose. The vice-president of marketing in a large corporation operates in a different sphere and has different concerns than the rising-star department head. Perhaps the most effective organizations are those that develop subnetworks. In these groups, women have an opportunity to find—or be—role models at various career levels, and to form alliances among their peers as well.

[1] Jane Wilson, "Networks," *Savvy* Magazine, January, 1980, p. 19.

TAPPING YOUR RESOURCES

There is nothing revolutionary about the idea of women helping one another. We have each built valuable support systems among our families and friends. There's the neighbor who keeps an eye on the house while we are gone on vacation; the friend who will pinch hit on days that the babysitter doesn't show. But many of us have been more reticent about asking for help in the professional arena. We feel uncomfortable. We think of it as exploitative.

This is nonsense. Think of it as resourceful.

Successful men have been doing it for years. To them, it comes as naturally as passing out business cards.

Suppose, for example, you have just spent a year on a committee, in your company, assigned to evaluating several kinds of word-processing equipment. You're talking about this at a dinner party and a few days later, you get a call from one of the guests who you met that evening. She works at a large law firm where she has been put in charge of updating equipment in the typing pool. She would like to know which machines you feel are most versatile and efficient.

Are you annoyed by this inquiry? Of course not. You're rather flattered.

And she is simply being expedient. Even if she still decides to test the machines herself, you have saved her some valuable time by giving her a basis for comparison.

Some day you may ask her to recommend a good attorney. Or she may remember you when she hears about a high-level job opening that just fits your skills and experience. But the point of networking is not to exchange favors on a quid pro quo basis. In fact, in the situation just described, you have already done *yourself* a favor by advancing your reputation as a friendly, approachable person willing to share your expertise.

None of us has time to become an expert in everything. We must rely freely on each other. I call on Liz, who keeps up with local politics, for background on a school board issue. Anne Marie, my friend in real estate, knows about housing market trends. Marlene spent three days in December reading and talking to people before investing in cross-country ski equipment; if I decide to take up the sport, I'll just talk to her.

Networking got many people I know their first job, and from there, progressively better jobs. In some instances, it can even create them.

Kathy, twenty-four, graduated from college with honors in art and music. She had done lots of volunteer work for the previous four years, organizing exhibits, concerts, and other events. Still, job offers in the fine arts were scarce in 1977, particularly since Kathy wanted to remain in the town where she had gone to school. Her friend Marilee, twenty-six, who had directed and staged several plays and musicals during her college days, was having a similar lack of success in the job market.

They pooled their contacts among local amateur actors and actresses, musicians, and media people, made arrangements with a local restaurant, and initiated a feature story in the local newspaper; soon, K & M Productions had launched a dinner theater with a four-week run of *The Fantasticks.* Later they branched out to a production of *Peter Pan* for children and a live music series called "Breakfast with Bach" on Sundays.

One of the most sophisticated uses of networking was reported in *Newsweek* magazine shortly after the 1980 presidential election. Senior White House Aide Anne Wexler had set up an "old girl network" to help find jobs for some of the record 450 top-level women President Jimmy Carter had brought into his administration, the magazine reported.

Wexler contacted executive-search firms and offered job resumes for women who had served in such positions as assistant cabinet secretary, general consul, and agency head. "Many corporations and universities don't realize what is available in Washington," Wexler said, "even as they search elsewhere. Men have an automatic network for tracking jobs. Women don't."[2]

I used networking to gather material for this book. My colleagues in Professional Women in Communications filled out a large share of my time-management surveys and passed them on to their friends in other parts of the country. The surveys came back with information and suggestions for new people to contact. At a regional conference for college and university public relations directors, my boss mentioned the book topic at a dinner table and I was instantly presented with names of time-management authorities from Penn State to Stanford University. I wrote to each of them and almost immediately received thick packets with more resource materials. My chain of information kept growing. When this book is published, I plan to plug into the same communication system for help in promoting it.

[2]"An Old-Girl Network for Carter Aides," *Newsweek,* December 22, 1980, p. 10.

YOU'VE GOT CONNECTIONS

Suppose a group of you want to start a formal women's network in your community or your company. Begin as you would in creating any new organization: Draw up a list of potential members; talk up the organization among yourselves; and set a time, date, and place for a brainstorming session.

At the brainstorming session, talk about the purpose and structure of your group. Should the membership be limited or open to everyone? How often will it meet, and with what sort of format? Begin formulating a statement of purpose.

Over the next three to four meetings, try to assess the degree of commitment among those in attendance. Keep in touch with women who seemed to support the idea but couldn't make it to the inital meetings; see if you can count on them in at least an advisory capacity. Project goals for your organization three months and six months down the road. Plan to periodically assess your goals and progress.

As with any meeting, designate someone to take notes and someone to type up and distribute a report to interested persons. Appoint a phone committee. As the group begins to take shape, you may decide to elect officers or form a steering committee.

Whether or not you decide to go the formal route of creating a women's network or joining one that is already established, rediscover the valuable contacts you already have. From your past: Friends and teachers from high school; acquaintances from a previous job or your old neighborhood. In your professional life: Co-workers, clients, people you meet at a conference or workshop. In your personal life: Extended family, good friends, fellow members of church and civic groups, even the members of your carpool. Each may be a resource for you, and you for them.

In networking it is who you are *and* who you know that counts.

Books on business politics have pointed out that one of the reasons for women's failure to rise in management is that as children, they learned to make "best friends," while little boys work at "making the team." Women's networks are a team. We may have assembled late in the season, but we're still in time for the playoffs.

9

Going Places

Have you heard the one about the traveling saleswoman?

Probably not, because she is taken very seriously, along with the woman conference delegate, lecturer, and consultant. The airline and hotel industries view professional women travelers as their fastest growing market, and accurately so. Eastern Airlines reported that women made some 28 million business trips by air alone in 1978, nearly twice as many as in 1977. United Airlines estimated that nearly one in five of its business travelers in 1979 were women.

Many of us may greet this form of job mobility with a mixture of exhilaration and uneasiness. Time management is trickier on the road; you may be faced with fitting a set of intensely important objectives into other people's schedules. You're putting yourself at the mercy of crazy cabdrivers and overbooked planes. Further, you're entering this unfamiliar territory without your support system: Your desk, your secretary, your family.

PREPARE IN ADVANCE

If you're a traveling parent, the first thing you may be dealing with is guilt. It's not easy traveling with kids, toys, and a diaper bag, but it's often harder to leave them behind. The telephone is a means of mutual reassurance that out of sight does not mean out of touch. Post detailed instructions for whoever is in charge while you're away, listing the phone numbers of the children's doctor, teacher, and at least two

71

adults who can serve as backups in case of an emergency. Leave your itinerary and the phone numbers where you can be reached at all hours, and agree on a time at which you yourself will call home daily.

If you're a single mother, see about hiring a friend or relative to "live in" with your children while you're out of town. One of your unmarried or child-free friends might welcome the chance to play surrogate parent. Or explore the possibility of trade-offs with other parents. They might be glad to take off for a weekend by themselves while their children visit you.

Evaluate carefully what you mean to accomplish. Is it worth the time away or can it be handled by someone else or by a series of phone calls? Once you decide that the trip has top priority, set up appointments with the people you need to see, and confirm them the day before. Leave at your office a copy of your itinerary and the phone numbers where you can always be reached. Check and recheck the materials you'll be bringing: Documents, hand-outs, notepaper, business cards. If you're making any kind of audio-visual presentation, make sure the equipment is in proper working order before you pack it. Don't rely on the word of the last person who used it.

By this time you should also have in hand confirmed reservations, including those for your plane, rental car, and hotel. A travel agent can help you secure tickets and book accommodations that meet your needs—such as proximity to your meeting place, an airline shuttle service, and perhaps a swimming pool.

PACK LIGHT

Make a list of what to bring and to wear a few days before you leave, checking to make sure that that pivotal dress in your wardrobe doesn't need cleaning. Aim for the fewest possible items—in wrinkle-free fabrics—that can be coordinated in several ways. Above all, don't bring more than you can carry by yourself.

The following should see you through a week of business and pleasure:

- Suit jacket or blazer
- Two skirts, one that matches the jacket and one that coordinates
- Shirtwaist dress, also matching the jacket
- Three drip-dry blouses or shirts

- Cocktail dress
- One pair of slacks or jeans, for off-hours; t-shirts or turtlenecks
- Lingerie (three sets); stockings, with spare pairs
- Sleepwear, swimsuit
- Belts, scarves, other accessories
- Dressy, business, and casual shoes

Pack your suitcase with shoes and other heavy items opposite the handle. Tuck soft things in and around them to conserve space. Roll your lingerie, sleepwear, and swimsuit, and put them at the bottom. Fold blouses, skirts, and other such items in thirds and overlap them so that each garment cushions the folds of the next. Wear your suit, and carry an all-weather coat.

In your carry-on case put anything spillable, breakable, or valuable, including cosmetics (in small plastic containers), jewelry, money, your alarm clock, and prescription medicines. Also put in your carry-on case important papers, such as your itinerary, lecture notes, and one set of any hand-outs you plan to distribute, so that if your checked luggage is delayed, you can still make copies. Tuck in one change of clothes as a similar precaution.

On a very brief trip, take everything in a single garment bag that can be stowed in the plane's coat compartment; you'll save waiting at the baggage claims area and eliminate any possibility of lost or misdirected luggage.

Two considerations in selecting a travel outfit are comfort and pockets. In the latter you can keep dollars and quarters so as to avoid fumbling through your purse for a tip.

If you're going to be traveling often, you might consider these investments:

- A credit card—to speed reservations and purchases, to keep a record of these transactions, and to reduce your reliance on cash. In fact, renting a car without a credit card is practically impossible.
- Special travel appliances, such as a compact hair dryer and curling iron, a clothes steamer or iron, and a one-cup coffee maker.
- An airline club membership—your passport to VIP lounges with comfortable chairs, television sets and newspapers, and meeting rooms.
- Wheels: Either built into your suitcase or in the form of a collapsible luggage cart.

BE A PROFESSIONAL

The key to assuring yourself good service and avoiding hassles as you travel is to be a professional. Project self-confidence in your dealings with airline and hotel personnel. If you don't get the room you requested, it is up to the hotel to find you comparable accommodations.

And speaking of rooms, it is a good security measure to request one near the elevator.

Keep scrupulous account—with all receipts—of your expenses, and tally them up immediately after you return. Don't rely on your memory to keep track of parking-lot fees, bellhop tips, and all the other little incidentals that could mount up to a rather sizable reimbursement.

Be direct and explicit with people you are meeting, and follow up your trip with a letter recapping any agreements that were reached. As a conference delegate, you may want to write an appreciative note to the person who organized the event. Send a memo to your boss, evaluating the success of your mission. And on your own, review what went smoothly or not, and why. Plan ways to make future trips even more productive.

Traveling on the job should be an enriching—not a frustrating—experience. Schedule a few free hours to duck into a museum or a distinguished restaurant. Reserve tickets for a tour or a cultural event. If you can spare an extra day or two at the beginning or end of the trip, take a mini-vacation. Maybe your family or a good friend can meet you to help your further exploration of the city you're visiting; maybe you can route yourself home via a weekend cruise.

Some booklets worth writing for are:

- "Fly Rights," from the Civil Aeronautics Board, 1825 Connecticut Ave., N.W., Washington, D.C., 20428. Free.
- "Tips for Travelers," from the American Hotel and Motel Association, 888 Seventh Ave., New York, N.Y. 11102. Free. (Enclose a stamped, self-addressed, legal-sized envelope.)
- "Ladies and Men's Packing Guide," from the Samsonite Corporation, 11200 E. 45th Ave., Denver, Co. 80239. Free.

Home Work

POSITION NOW OPEN

Flexible hours. Unlimited earnings. Infinite growth
potential. Cozy work atmosphere
with all the comforts of home.

It seems like the perfect solution. The best of both worlds.

Here you are with this adorable new baby; child-care costs a fortune, and you don't want to leave her with anyone else anyway. You've
always been good at—(gourmet cooking, typing, dog grooming, you
name it)—and you've always wanted to try doing it for profit.

Or here you are, fed up with a job that has zero mobility and less
challenge. You're tired of seeing the profits of your hard work filling
the company coffers instead of your own. Why do you need the company to back you? You have some money saved, plenty of energy and
ambition, and some contacts of your own.

Either way, the time seems right to strike out on your own and see
what happens. And so you should!

But first, do some research. Consider:

- What have I got going for me? Am I extremely self-disciplined? Can I rely
  on myself to take charge of a project and see it through to completion?
- What is the market for my talent or product? Are many other people in
  town doing the same thing? How much are they charging for it? Is there a
  repeat demand for it?

- How can I promote it? How do I gain publicity in the media? Access to stores, craft fairs, and other sales outlets? Do I relate well to just about everybody?
- Am I in this for the money? Or am I in it because I really love what I am planning to do? In either case, how much money do I have to make to justify the effort?

Before you sink your time, energy, and cash into any business venture, talk to people who have done it. Your potential competitors probably won't open their books to you, but a local entrepreneur with a comparable business may be glad to advise you on such matters as overhead costs, insurance, equipment, and other expenses; someone operating your type of business in another city may be glad to do the same.

The Small Business Administration district office in your area offers some 200 pamphlets on all aspects of business management, along with workbooks for keeping financial accounts. The SBA also conducts seminars on setting up businesses, and provides assistance on applying for loans. (For a free list of SBA district offices and publications, request forms SBA 115A and SBA 115B from the Small Business Administration, Washington, D.C. 20416.)

Is there a women-business-owners group in your community that you could network with? Any trade magazines you might subscribe to? Seek advice from many sources. Read all you can. Dispel your fantasies and start with a solid plan of action.

IS IT REALLY FOR YOU?

When my husband started his own computer-software business ten years ago, I saw it as freedom from the forty-hour work week. (He was soon working closer to eighty.) No boss telling him what to do. (He had to do everything.) Freedom to take a five-week cross-country vacation. (Leave your own business for five weeks? Who was I kidding? If it can run without you for five weeks, there can't be much business.) And as for money, which I thought would come in like a tidal wave, we learned that accounts receivable cannot be applied to the utility bill.

My husband is still running his own business (it's expanded now, with employees and a separate office), and I still have very positive, but less romanticized, feelings about it. I have learned from his experience, from the experiences of self-employed women I've interviewed, and from my own stint as a freelance writer when I was between jobs that it takes lots of self-discipline to achieve success. You've got to be a self-starter. You must be willing to take risks. And time-management skills are not just advantageous; they're indispensable!

Nancy, thirty-six, is a California artist who has effectively integrated her professional and personal lives. She puts a premium on time by herself, and uses it creatively, whether painting batiks to sell at an upcoming art fair, filling orders for a San Francisco gift shop, or brewing soup. She puts in regular hours each week for her artwork, housework, family, and social activities. Each sphere of her life balances and enhances the other.

In contrast, I recall my days of magazine writing and editing at home after my daughter was born. I was twenty-five and after three hectic years of newspaper reporting I was ready for this change of pace. Freelancing was just what I'd always wanted to do.

I had no trouble getting assignments. Within weeks I was busy on several magazine pieces, writing a weekly newspaper column, and stringing for the *Detroit News*. But it was lonely! I learned that sitting at a typewriter for ten hours a day (babies sleep a lot during the early months) is grueling. Once I had longed for a quiet place to work without ringing phones and rattling typewriters. Now I missed the camaraderie of the office, even the overlong staff meetings and other interruptions.

For me, the solitary nature of working at home was too much of a good thing. I found out that I prefer a job with more structure and social contact. (And I do not mind such amenities as health insurance, vacations, and a regular paycheck). But I'm glad that I tried it. The attempt removed "full-time freelancing" from my "lifelong ambition" list, and sent it over to my growing store of "valuable learning experiences."

MAKING IT SUCCEED

If you're currently working at home or considering it for the future, be aware that the very factors that make it so appealing are the same ones that make it difficult. Here's how to turn those elements to your advantage.

Flexible hours

Pretend they're not. Resolve to work a certain number of hours per day, just as you would at an office, and stick to your schedule. Know your energy cycle (see Chapter 2) and plan your work hours to coincide with the times when you feel refreshed and productive. Inform your friends of your working hours so they won't drop in on you—unless it's on business. If phone calls prove disruptive, consider hiring an answering service or installing a tape-recording answering machine.

Also, know when to quit. During the early days of starting a new business you may feel so motivated and so full of energy and enthusiasm that you find it absorbing *all* of your time, seven days a week. This may be desirable while you're getting established, but it's unhealthy to let it go on indefinitely. Nobody's paying you time-and-a-half, you know. Schedule time off to enjoy the fruits of your labors.

Bernice, who does sewing and alterations at home, has a problem separating work and personal time because "the work is always within reach. With a constant backlog of orders to fill, I feel I should be productive every minute. If I'm watching the 11 o'clock news and I'm not hemming a skirt at the same time, I feel guilty about it."

But she adds, "Right now I'm building a clientele. I feel I have to keep my prices low to be competitive and therefore I have to work longer hours to cover expenses. As I get established, I plan to be more selective in the jobs I accept. I'll be able to choose more interesting, exacting projects and name my fee—because the customers will know I do quality work."

Unlimited Earnings

While you may be dreaming of your income in terms of "the sky is the limit," it is more realistic to think about "meeting expenses." Even that may take several years. Business owners I've talked to recommend that you plan on a minimum of six months (and eighteen is better) before expecting your business to improve your standard of living. (All this depends, of course, on the kind of business you've begun.) Besides, you will probably want to reinvest your profit—in inventory, advertising, and eventually, perhaps, in hired help.

Self employment teaches you great respect for the adage "time is money."

"In fact, you can become obsessed with it," remarks Margo, who owns her own writing, editing, and photography business. "When I'm calling on a potential client and he leans back in his chair and begins telling me about his early days in business, I want to choke him. I don't have time to listen to stories! I need to be out contracting new business, and if he's not going to commission any, I shouldn't be spending even ten minutes with him!

"When you're working for someone else, you get paid just to *be* there," she observes, "but in business for yourself, you've got to make every minute count. I group errands to coincide with when I'm going to be in a certain area of town, and fit social contacts around business calls. I know this sounds compulsive but the business is exciting and rewarding to me right now, so I go with it."

It feels good, Bernice and Margo agree, to see the money come in direct proportion to the energy expended. It's *better* than a weekly paycheck because you feel in control of your income. But this can be addictive. When your skills are in demand, it is tempting to overcommit yourself. Suddenly there you are, back behind the eight ball. When your business begins running *you* instead of vice-versa, it's time to step back and review why you started it in the first place. Work should enhance your life, not consume it.

Cozy work atmosphere

The women I know who work from their homes say it's essential to create a separate space for business only; a place where you can leave your work spread out, so that you can pick up where you left off. A spare room, the garage, or the basement is ideal. A desk or work table is minimal.

Even then, you may find it hard to separate yourself psychologically from those things you associate with household routine. Your eyes roam. You notice a big handprint on the mirror. Can you really resist jumping up and cleaning it until the end of your self-imposed work day?

"I find it works best to physically remove yourself from the house," says Nancy. "I rent a studio with two other women artists. It's an added expense, but it acknowledges that we take our work seriously. And it may be that we work more diligently because we're aware of the overhead.''

Unlimited growth potential

Among all the special attributes of running your own business, growth may be the area hardest to control. And, like those features mentioned earlier, it has both advantages and drawbacks.

Analyze your product or service carefully. Will one sale lead to another and create a stable of repeat customers? Or could your idea be a fad that will peak and plummet? Twelve waterbed outlets emerged in our community within a six-month period back in the early seventies. Within the following six months, all but two were out of business.

On the other side, are you prepared for success?

My sister-in-law Sue came up with an idea for ''plant parties'' as a home business. One person invited a group of friends over, and Sue arrived at the hostess's home with a carload of potted house plants. She told the gathering how to care for the various varieties and then took orders from the guests. She arranged to buy the plants wholesale from area nurseries and priced them at a small markup. Each party led to new bookings, and on some evenings, Sue found herself addressing groups of twenty-five to forty people. She was soon spending every night of the week talking about plants and all day trucking around delivering them. The project mushroomed out of control and she decided to drop it and do something different.

Some business owners I know resist expansion because they prefer to spend their time doing, not administering.

Caren began a successful nursery school in her own home when her children were small. As the enrollment and her reputation grew, Caren was repeatedly approached about franchising the school. ''How could I be sure of maintaining the quality if I did that?'' she wondered. ''I'd be spending all my time with bookkeeping and personal matters, when what I really want to do is work with the children!'' She decided to maintain just one school, with which she could preserve personal contact.

On the other hand, Paula, working from her home as sales representative for a printing company, purposefully hired a secretary and trained her to handle routine sales contacts and follow-up paperwork.

Her secretary is now "more of an assistant," Paula says, "able to do everything I did at the beginning." She, in turn, is free to move on to contact new clients and nail down new business.

The advantage of being your own boss is that you, to a considerable degree, can determine how far you want to go. That is not to say that you won't be subject to economic and market trends, but there are plenty of variables that are within your control. Your energy, skills, and strategic use of time are valuable resources.

Your success in the final analysis isn't measured by the size of your business, income, prestige, or any other conventional standards as much as by the satisfaction you gain from the experience.

Order in the House

When Elsa was a bride in 1947, her husband offered to hire a maid to help her with the housework. "Not necessary," she replied, but agreed to accept a household budget that would cover such an expense in case she changed her mind in the future. Then Elsa opened a savings account and every week, over the next thirty years, paid herself for running the house. She set wages in accordance with those charged by other professionals, and gave herself regular raises and bonuses. She paid herself for the twenty-five quarts of tomatoes she canned one summer and the set of dining room chairs she refinished one winter. By the time she was sixty she had financed four trips to Europe, a stock portfolio, and a condominium in Florida.

The point of this story is not that there are big bucks to be made in housework. Rather, it illustrates the importance of attitude. Housework is serious business, too often underrated both by those who do it and by those who benefit from it. It demands organization, management skills, creativity, and industriousness.

Dirt can be depressing, but a clean, orderly environment is uplifting and gives impetus to the rest of your tasks. Its value is both economic and psychic. Open spaces are healthier, more maneuverable, and lots more attractive than clutter. Housework may indeed be boring, unrewarding, and difficult, but don't ever call it unimportant.

Whether you're at home full time, at a full-time job, or split between the two, it is likely that nine times out of ten you are doing most of the housework, or at least feeling responsible for it. If you're single, you're responsible ten times out of ten. Acknowledging the unfairness of this situation, we will hold all complaints for Chapter 19. To drift into a treatise on sex role stereotypes at this point would avert our basic purpose—to get the job done.

Consider for now the advantages of running a household. You get to call the shots, set your own standards, and decide what's important. So instead of feeling oppressed, seize the responsibility. Take advantage of being in charge.

GETTING IT ALL TOGETHER

The first step is to organize the house or apartment with the proverbial "place for everything and everything in its place." You may associate this principle with your compulsive aunt who positioned the same china frog on the same walnut table in the same corner for twenty years, but I'm talking about *interior* space: the grouping together of similar objects so that they can be instantly stored and found again. It's an imperative first step—a lesson I've learned after losing weeks of my life, cumulatively, hunting for missing shoes, library books, and the only set of car keys.

You probably already adhere to two basic tenets of household organization: That things should be kept as close as possible to the place of their use, and that the most frequently used things should be the most accessible. Thus, the drawer nearest the dining area contains eating utensils; the everyday flatware is handily in the divider tray in front, while the punch bowl ladle rests in the rear. The same rule applies to all storage areas, from the hall closet to the refrigerator.

As you begin putting everything in order, you'll probably notice a disparity between your mountain of possessions and your molehill of storage space; this is not your cue to build an addition to the house.

The fewer things you own, the easier they'll be to organize. So gather up a couple of large cardboard boxes for recyclable items, a big plastic bag for the garbage, and *eliminate.* Tackle one small space at a time; a drawer or a closet is less intimidating than the entire basement. Be ruthless. Tell yourself you're not parting with valuables, but gaining fresh, free space.

Stephanie Winston, founder and director of a consulting agency called The Organizing Principle, tells her clients to consider each item individually and ask themselves:

> Have I used this article in the past year? If not,
> Does it have sentimental or monetary value to me?
> Might it come in handy some day?

If you can say yes only to the third question, start pitching.[1]

Those things that are "still good" (like the wool miniskirt you were going to alter to fit your daughter—who, however, now only wears blue jeans) will be welcomed by the local thrift shop or the church clothing drive. Pass the eleven volumes of *National Geographic* on to the public library. You can always check out the issue on Nova Scotia again if you really want to reread it.

Still feeling possessive? Give yourself a cash incentive along with a deadline: Hold a garage sale. We hold a mammoth "multi-family yard sale" once a year, inviting neighbors to contribute, and marking the neighbors' initials on a removable price sticker attached to the merchandise they bring. When the item is sold, the sticker is removed to a page of paper that has the family's name on it—an effortless method of bookkeeping. Everyone chips in to pay for an attention-grabbing newspaper ad, and to make large posters with directional arrows at eight nearby intersections.

Increasingly, these sales are conducted by the kids. They get good practice in math and merchandising as they tally up purchases and make change. It's also a good way to reform the juvenile packrat ("do you really want this doll buggy or would you rather sell it and earn money toward a new bike?").

Keep all prices low and negotiable. Since your main goal is to free yourself of these burdensome belongings, you can view any cash you take in as a windfall profit.

[1]Stephanie Winston, *Getting Organized* (New York: W.W. Norton and Company, Inc. 1978), p. 123.

STRETCHING YOUR STORAGE

Once you've pared down your possessions to the things you really need and use, fix up your storage space so that everything is easy to latch onto. You'll find many do-it-yourself storage ideas in magazines such as *Better Homes and Gardens* and in the home-improvement section of your library or bookstore. Then check out your local hardware store for the latest easy-to-install equipment.

Walls

These may be your most under-utilized resource for keeping handy and visible the things you use most often. If yours are merely holding the roof up, consider the added advantages of:

A pegboard: Sturdy and versatile, this allows you to hang large items like mops and brooms in the utility closet or along the stairs to the basement. A pegboard near the stove can support heavy skillets and other cooking equipment.

A corkboard: This comes in sections, with or without adhesive backing for easy installation. One or more squares make a perfect message center near the desk or telephone; alternatively, you can use it to cover a wall in a child's room and display posters, photographs, and school art work.

Shelving: This can be made to fit any space. You can buy vertical metal tracks and place prefinished boards across the adjustable brackets that fit into the tracks, changing the height of the shelves as needed for whatever-size objects the shelves are to accommodate. Or buy L-shaped metal brackets, either utilitarian or decorative, and have boards cut to size at the lumberyard.

Shelves can fit into many odd places—alongside your kitchen counter, perhaps, to clear the toaster and other appliances off your work space. Insert wood triangles, of graduated size, in a corner for built-in knick-knack shelves. A strip of wood just under the windowsill is perfect for a row of plants. And a shelf about twenty-four inches from the ceiling could be used to display a collection of large baskets, which in turn can be used to store smaller items.

Hooks, hatracks, carpentry nails, and *clothespins*: These should get everything else you use frequently off the floor and out where you can see it. Hanging space should be reserved for the things you use most often. First decide what to hang, and then where it will be most accessible. For objects more functional than decorative (the dog leash, the shower cap), make use of the insides of doors and the wall space just inside the closet. Some ideas: A row of nails on a wall in the bedroom can be used for scarves, belts, necklaces, and other accessories. Spring-type clothespins glued to a strip of wood are perfect for hanging purses or mittens. A bicycle basket, since it's flat on one side, can be hung against the wall to hold the day's mail.

Drawers

Drawers are your main means of clutter control. The more you have the better, because with lots of compartments, you can keep each group of items systematically separate. If you're planning to buy any new piece of furniture, pick the model with the most drawer space.

Some objects, such as stationery and envelopes, stack themselves neatly and snugly inside a drawer; others, like your kitchen gadgets, can only be stored in a jumble. For these, buy a plastic drawer divider or improvise, using an ice tray or small cardboard boxes, to keep the things you use most often on top and in front. A sliding tray, available at the hardware store, is even better because it gives a deep drawer an upper and lower deck.

If you're short on drawer space, relegate some of the things you use less regularly to special baskets or boxes that can be stored on shelves. These might include sewing and mending supplies; shoeshine bottles and brushes; and your assortment of gift wrap, tags, ribbon, and string. As for paper cups, plates, and the thermos, store them right in the picnic basket.

Cupboards

Cupboards that are especially high or deep needn't contain wasted space if you insert one or more free-standing shelves along the side. One manufacturer makes several sizes that stack one on top of the other. You can also install a plastic slide-out drawer underneath one of the cupboard shelves, or a special rack to hang wine glasses or coffee cups. Screw a small utility rack to the inside wall or door of the cupboard under the sink for sponges and pot scrubbers. Put odd-lot items that you don't use often—like that collection of half empty bottles of liqueur—in the rear of a deep cupboard, on a lazy susan.

Closets

These can be improved with the addition of shelves, hooks, or a second clothes rod. Scrutinize all your closets and pockets of wasted space. In the bedroom, for example, put a shelf above the clothes-pole for sweaters or extra blankets. Hang a shoe bag and belt hooks on the door. Insert a small chest or stacking bins beneath your hanging blouses to consolidate hosiery, scarves, and other accessories.

In the remaining rooms or hallways you probably have a linen closet, a coat closet, and a utility closet, but never mind their intended uses. Fit them to meet your needs. If the shelves in the linen closet best accommodate the movie projector and your eighty reels of vacation footage, fine. Sheets and towels can be stowed in a chest.

Key your closet use to the season, too. In the winter, put coats in the coat closet. In summer, store the coats at the drycleaners and free up the closet for the tennis racket and swim-fins.

In the utility closet (or whatever space you use for one—perhaps one section of the garage), hang the broom, sponge mop, dustpan, and so forth off the floor, so that they don't collect extra dirt. Install shelves about eight inches deep along the wall for cleansers, the iron, and other supplies. Surplus shelf space in a closet may come in handy as extra pantry space. Collect some large, sturdy boxes from the supermarket for storing vacuum attachments, bottles to be recycled, rags, and other miscellaneous items.

Functional Furnishings

These can provide extra storage for those items that didn't quite fit into your carefully planned scheme of closets, drawers, and shelf containers; indeed, anyone who lives in a pre-Civil-War house, as I do, has learned that closets are a luxury, not an entitlement. One can invest in a magnificent antique wardrobe or Hoosier cupboard to hold the overflow, but there are less expensive alternatives:

- A zip-open floor-pillow cover can hold extra pillows and quilts.
- An old footlocker or wicker trunk is of ideal height to serve as a coffee table, while providing volumes of storage space.
- A lift-top piano bench can be used for hiding away flat items, such as magazines, placemats, or even sheet music—of all things—while serving as a window seat or plant stand.
- A big laundry-type basket is indispensable for end-of-the-day and emergency cleanups. The clutter is tossed inside and the basket is stashed in a spare room. Each family member is responsible for retrieving his or her belongings from the basket by morning.
- Keep another basket by the doorway to collect lunchpails, books, homework, and the like when the kids come home from school. This keeps them from cluttering up the kitchen counter, where you'd planned to fix dinner.
- Use suitcases for storing off-season clothing.
- Shove suitcases or other flat boxes of stored items under the beds.

CONTROL CENTRAL

Whether you're operating from a fourteen-room mansion or a studio apartment, you need one cozy corner for conducting household and personal business, maintaining files, and storing supplies. Here's the spot for your desk or whatever piece of furniture you can improvise into a desk; be sure you have an ample writing surface, drawers, and a shelf or ledge for the phone book, dictionary, and other frequently used reference books. An old Victorian rolltop desk provides lots of compartments and cubbyholes, plus a top that can be closed to hide work-in-progress. For a more contemporary look, put a butcherblock across two file cabinets.

Equip your "home office" with:

- Plenty of ballpoint pens, felt-tip pens, pencils, and a pencil sharpener
- Cellophane tape, paper clips, a stapler, rubber bands, and glue
- Scissors, a ruler, a clipboard, and scratch pads
- Business and personal stationery, extra envelopes, a supply of greeting cards, gummed labels, and stamps
- If you type, typing paper, carbon paper, and correction papers or fluid
- Optional assets include a postal scale, a staple remover, and a calculator

Within or near your self-contained "control central" you'll keep the tools described in Chapter 5: Your ongoing To-Do list, your personal planning calendar (which travels with you to and from your job), your household activities calendar, and your file system. If you spend much time on the telephone, an extension line here is essential.

Finally, we will make a quick tour of those rooms that are fastest to self-destruct:

A child's room: This should be organized so that the child can take care of his or her own things. Arrange clothing in drawers in the same order in which the child gets dressed: Underwear on top; shirts second; pants third; socks, sweaters, and pajamas on the bottom. If the upper drawers are beyond the child's reach, use them for off-season storage. Install a low clothes rod in the closet so that the child can put things on and off hangers without help. Give the child a personal laundry hamper, or acquaint the child with the family system (see Chapter 13).

Relegate large, bulky toys to the toy box, and small items, such as Lego pieces, puzzle pieces, doll clothes, and the like into small containers such as plastic dishpans, empty coffee cans (with tape to cover any sharp edges on the inside rim), and cylindrical cardboard ice cream containers. A tool or tackle box is perfect for consolidating art supplies, with the trays and compartments being used to hold scissors, paste, crayons, and so forth. Provide a few open shelves for books and special toys and, of course, a generous waste basket.

The bed will be easiest to make if it's positioned away from the wall. If this is impractical—either because the room is too small or because the child sleeps with 105 stuffed animals, push the bed against the wall and eliminate bedmaking altogether: Substitute a comforter or a slumber bag for the sheets and blankets. In the morning, the comforter or bag can just be rolled up and tucked away.

The bathroom: The bathroom will take care of itself if you invoke the following rule: Each person leaves it as he or she finds it. This means swishing the globs of toothpaste out of the sink after toothbrushing; re-straightening the towels; wiping around the toilet as necessary, and scrubbing away the bathtub ring. Keep a can of cleanser and a sponge handy—behind the shower curtain perhaps, or under the sink.

To conserve storage space, try stacking folded towels on open shelves, all the way to the ceiling. They'll be both convenient and colorful. Shower caddies for soap, a shower cap, and a washrag are available in a number of designs, and hook conveniently over the shower rod; or you can consolidate the shampoo, bath oil, toy boat, and other paraphernalia in a plastic bucket (which can also serve for hair rinsing) and stash it out of sight.

The next time you're supervising your toddler's bath, clean out the medicine chest. Throw out all of the outdated prescription bottles, the mascara that made your eyes water, the unopened aftershave your husband received three Christmases ago. Organize the shelves by categories—first-aid, hygiene, make-up, and so forth—and remove any pills or poisonous liquids to a "medicine box" that can be put out of reach of children.

Instead of covering up a chipped toilet seat with one of those fuzzy toilet, tank, and bathmat sets, which have to be washed and fluff-dried regularly to make them look nice, note that with a simple screwdriver you can just replace the seat. New seats come in bright colors, in woodfinishes, and even in cushioned vinyl.

Finally, hang a few plants. They'll thrive in the humidity created by frequent showers, and will divert attention from the less interesting fixtures in the room. With the faucet only a few feet away, you'll never forget to water them.

The kitchen: The kitchen is your most functional room, whether the hours you spend bent over a hot stove are blissful or torturous.

Your idea of a dream kitchen may be a long, clean countertop flanked by forty-eight symmetrical cupboards and drawers, with every potholder and paring knife tucked out of sight, leaving an unspoiled landscape of Formica and chrome.

This kitchen scores ten on tidiness but about one on efficiency. As a practical matter, it's better to have the tools you use most often out and within reach. You'll save time twice, by being able to instantly spot what you need and by just as quickly being able to put it back where it belongs.

Before I bought a pot rack, for instance, I had to grope through the cupboard for the right-sized skillet, which was usually nesting third from the bottom, behind the soup kettle. Now I just grab the correct pan from the rack, and when I'm done, rinse it and hang it to air dry. Some people argue that hanging pots in plain sight *costs* you time because you must keep them shiny and spotless. Admittedly I am not that compulsive. I simply hang their blackened bottoms facing the wall. No one has ever inspected them.

The pot rack proved so convenient that I installed a second rack for graters, measuring cups and spoons, the egg beater, and other utensils. Racks are available and adaptable for practically anything you'd care to hang, from dish towels to food-processor blades. If you need something handy, hang it. If it hasn't got a hanging hole, drill one.

Near the stove, keep a crock for spatulas, stirring spoons, and wire wisks. On the counter or open shelves, you could add canisters or Mason jars for flour, coffee, pasta, or other staples. Also line up the spice bottles you use regularly—but not on the stove where the heat will alter their flavor.

A knife block not only protects your knife blades, but also protects you against slicing your fingers while rummaging through a drawer. A magnetic bar, like the one in the garage for screwdrivers or drill bits, can be used to mount the bottle opener, vegetable peeler, and other lightweight gadgets.

If you prefer to organize all this equipment against one wall, a metal grid system or pegboard with hooks enables you to move items around at will. The wall area behind the stove might accommodate this. And the gap between the top of your cupboards and the ceiling might hold larger items, such as the salad bowl.

By now you may be thinking that the kitchen looks a bit cluttered. Think of it instead as friendly and functional. Who is to say that an artfully hung eggbeater isn't every bit as decorative, in its own way, as Waterford crystal.

The principles discussed earlier in this chapter on organizing drawers and cupboards apply to all interior kitchen space. To review:

- Assign top drawers and eye-level cabinet shelves as prime storage spaces. Put everything that is used most often toward the top and the front (unless it can be more conveniently hung on the wall).
- Use the inside doors of cupboards and pantry cabinets for mounting necessary but nonornamental items, like the paper towel dispenser, or for hanging dish rags.
- Keep everything as near as possible to its place of use. Scouring pads and dishwashing soap go under the sink; magnetized potholders attach to the stove, and so on.

- Store heavy items, such as cast iron skillets, on lower shelves; it's easier to lift them up than down.
- If, after finally organizing everything in order of usefulness, there is no space left for, say, the turkey roaster, wrap it in a plastic bag and store it in the garage or the attic.

Organize your food supply too, so that you know at a glance what is running low. Group together the soups; the canned vegetables; the condiments; boxed mixes; and so on. An empty three-pound coffee can or a shoe box is handy for consolidating small packets of dry soups, salad dressing mixes, yeast, instant sauces, and the like. To expand your food storage space further, use a multi-tiered turntable, free-standing shelves, or a "kangaroo shelf" that hooks onto the bottom of one shelf and forms another. Expand your food-preparation space with a chopping board that fits across the sink.

Take advantage of time savers such as food processors, crock-pots, pressure cookers, and microwave ovens, but resist the temptation to amass lots of silly, single-purpose gadgets like shish-kabob roasters and donut machines. They're bulky to store and rarely perform any operation that isn't just as easily done on the stove.

The objective is a kitchen that is streamlined and functional, geared to your specific cooking needs. If you enjoy making breads and pastries, organize a baking center, with the flour and sugar canisters, your rolling pin, measuring tools, and so forth close at hand. If stir-fry cooking is your thing, allocate prime space to the wok—maybe storing it right inside the oven. With new products being developed continuously to expand your workspace and improve cooking procedures, your kitchen can become the most revolutionary and efficient room in your action-ready house.

True Grit

Now that your belongings have been systematically sorted out, scaled down, and set in order, you're no doubt anxious to get on with cleaning them.

Dirt takes a variety of forms. In the bathroom it appears as charcoal-grey speckles of mildew around the shower stall. In the kitchen it's yesterday's spilled orange juice. By removing these disfigurements on a routine, regular basis, we prevent them from reaching the advanced stage known as filth. Here is a four-pronged plan of attack:

The 30-minutes-a-day clean sweep. Your kitchen can be as hygenic as a surgical ward, but no one will notice if you haven't cleared the breakfast dishes. On the other hand, no one will spy grimy baseboards if the counters are clean; therefore, on a day-to-day basis, just keep after the clutter. This consists mainly of picking up, putting away, wiping, and straightening out. If your schedule permits, you might put in ten minutes of this activity before leaving for work in the morning, so that the house looks inviting on your return. Get everyone in the family to pitch in, of course. Make it a precondition to sitting down to dinner or switching on the television.

The once-a-week washout. Usually on a Saturday morning, so that you can spend the rest of the weekend in a pleasant environment, strip and change the beds; dust; sweep, damp mop, or vacuum the floors; catch the blatant finger smears on mirrors, walls, or windows; shake out rugs; and so on. It's mainly the *surfaces* you're after, with the floors probably requiring the most effort.

If it is reasonably tidy to begin with, an average-sized three-bedroom house should take under three hours to clean. Put the kids in charge of their own rooms and assign them other duties while you concentrate on the areas of the house that most need attention. Make a game of working as fast as possible, trying each week to top your best record. Set a deadline for finishing and if you're not done, quit anyway. Start next week where you left off this week.

The company's coming crash clean-up. Unlikely as it seems, you have fallen behind in your daily clutter control and some friends have just called to say they're passing through town. You figure it will take them twenty minutes to reach your place from the expressway. Don't panic.

Starting in the living room, gather up all toys, books, and other debris in a plastic laundry basket and haul it into the bedroom. Shut the door. Return to straighten newspapers, to empty ash trays, and to plump the couch and chair cushions. Save vacuuming until you've finished the next two rooms, if there's time left.

In the bathroom, straighten towels, sponge out the sink, put out a fresh bar of soap. Take a wad of wet toilet paper and wipe around the bathtub and toilet, then flush the paper. Close the shower curtain.

In the kitchen, clear all dishes into the sink or the dishwasher. Wipe the table and counter tops. Sweep and spot-clean the floor. Move your showiest house plant to the center of the kitchen table. Put on water for tea or coffee.

Finally, put on a clean shirt and check your hair and makeup. They were coming to see you, not the house, remember?

The semi-annual grand purge. Twice a year, or more often if necessary, hold a mass clean-up. Commit a long weekend or a series of two- to four-hour sessions to a repeat of the sorting and organizing process described in Chapter 11. It will amaze you how many things that seemed indispensable at last assessment now look useless and cumbersome. Pack them into a box for the next garage sale or giveaway, along with surplus magazines and outgrown clothing.

Do major cleaning jobs as necessary: Wash the inside and outside windows; clean out the refrigerator, freezer, and oven; wash the curtains and bedspreads; turn the mattresses; send slipcovers to be dry cleaned; shampoo the rugs.

You'll notice that the preceding formula emphasizes time-frames, not tasks. The specific chores mentioned are intended as examples of what you *might* do, not what you must do. A schedule should be an aid, not a straitjacket. Whatever routine you evolve, consider these principles:

- Housework expands to fill the time allotted to it. Therefore, to get it done more quickly, leave as little time for it as possible.
- The most frustrating aspect of housework is that it has to be done over again—later today, tomorrow, next week, or within the year. So occasionally, skip something that will have to be done again today or tomorrow and finish something that only needs to be done once a year.
- Go mainly for the clutter. The house will be more maneuverable and restful if things are picked up and put away, surfaces are clear, and so forth.
- Don't dust, vacuum, or wipe any surface until it looks dirty. Don't wax the floor if you can get by with damp mopping. Don't mop the floor if it just needs to be swept.
- Don't adhere to a schedule (Monday: laundry; Tuesday: baking; and the like) Do things according to necessity, not rigid routine.
- *Never* feel guilty if you let things slide. A clean house is desirable, not mandatory. In the final analysis it still belongs among your lowest priorities, well below your career, health, recreation, and personal relationships.

When you find a system that works for you, go with it. Develop your own standards, your own style. Many people find the best way to motivate themselves for a housecleaning is to invite friends over. Planning a party creates both an incentive and a deadline for getting the house in order. Others, in the tradition of an old-fashioned barn-raising, invite friends beforehand and make a party of cleaning the house. Some women I know insist that housecleaning in the nude is both pleasurable and practical (watch for the sequel to this book, which will be called *The Sensuous Housewife*). And although most people reserve their grubbiest clothes for housework, Sharon, a thirty-three year-old mother of four, uses a reverse tactic. "When the house is really a mess, I take a shower, put on a clean T-shirt and slacks, curl my hair, and put on make-up. Then I say to myself, 'What's a nice looking person like you doing in a crummy place like this?' And I get to work."

TOOLS

Cleaning supplies should be stored close to their place of use, so that whenever you're seized with a mad impulse to wipe peanut butter off the upstairs light switch, you won't have to trundle all the way down to the kitchen for a rag. Keep a set of the basics, such as cleanser, glass cleaner, paper towels, and a sponge in each of the bathrooms, and an extra dust rag in the living room and bedrooms. Consolidate additional cleaning supplies in a plastic caddy for the weekly room-by-room clean-up. And of course, if you have preschool children store the supplies safely out of reach.

Manufacturers have come out with so many special-purpose cleaning agents that you could spend an entire morning switching back and forth between carpet deodorizer, stain remover for stainless steel, and chrome foam, while carefully coordinating the fragrances—lemon oil, herbal essence, and disinfectant pine. A good argument can be made for settling on one good all-purpose cleaning liquid—perhaps one you concoct yourself from water and baking soda.

On the other hand, greasy embedded dirt often requires stronger stuff, and you can save yourself some scouring and scrubbing with a can of abrasive cleaner, such as Ajax. Experiment, and go with whatever seems to work best for you, whether it's your grandmother's secret formula of kerosene and rubbing alcohol, or scrubbing bubbles in a commercial spray can.

The other basic cleaning tools you need are a broom and dustpan; a whisk broom for awkward crevices such as those under the chair cushions and inside the car; a wet-mop with a detachable head that can be run through the washing machine when it gets grey and crusty; dust-and general-purpose rags, best made from old diapers and t-shirts; and paper towels, sponges, and brushes, including old toothbrushes for cleaning the grout between tiles.

To keep a vacuum cleaner working at top efficiency, change the bag frequently, and clean the brushes; if you have a canister model, you can use the suction hose to clean the brushes. Choose an upright model if what you mainly have to clean is carpeting, and a canister model if you have mainly tile or wood floors.

Some optional timesavers include a sponge mop; a pail, if the areas you are mopping are not near the sink; a squeegee, such as the ones service stations use for washing windows; a feather duster or its synthetic counterpart, for catching cobwebs around the ceiling and light fixtures; and a hand-held miniature vacuum cleaner, with batteries or a long cord, for quick cleanups, like cookie crumbs on the couch. Better yet, make a rule against eating on the couch.

Stick with these basics and forego the bulky, single-purpose appliances such as the electric floor waxers and rug shampooers—they can be rented once a year or so, when you need them. So, for that matter, can be the people who run them.

HIRING HELP

The best labor-saving device on the market is another person who will do your housework for you. Is it worth the expense? As usual, it depends on your priorities, and which is more valuable to you at the moment, your time or your money. If:

- You've been taking on more and more demanding responsibilities ouside the home;
- Your income has also increased;
- You'd rather spend your few free hours romping with your five-year-old than with the Rinse 'n' Vac....

Household help sounds like a timely and practical investment.

But finding it can be a little more complicated. The ideal housekeeper, like the ideal babysitter, is someone who is already employed by a friend or neighbor and thus comes with a built-in set of references. If no such person is available (or they're booked solid) check with an employment service or the part-time placement service at your local high school or college. Check your newspaper's "Situations Wanted" section or place an ad yourself. It needn't say more than "Housecleaning, X hours per week," and your phone number. The details can be explained when the applicants call.

To save their time and yours, do as much prescreening as possible. Over the phone, outline the specific jobs you have in mind and the days, hours, and wages for the work. Find out about each applicant's experience and the reasons for their having left previous jobs. Check out references before setting up a personal interview. Since only experience will show whether the people you'll see are competent, look for such qualities as reliability, enthusiasm, and cheerfulness.

It may take some weeks to see if the work is being done to your expectations. If you have some uncertainties suggest a one-month trial period (understanding also that the employee has the option of leaving you after that time too). Most housework is charged by the hour and not by the task, so, each time the cleaning person comes, leave a list of the jobs you need done, in order of their importance.

In figuring what this will cost you, don't forget to discuss transportation, lunch, social security, and, if you locate your employee through an agency, a finder's fee. An alternative to this is the cleaning service, which usually sends a team of people through your house for a specific job or for a specified time period; it is more impersonal (which may be your preference) and more expensive, but possibly more satisfactory.

Having a maid, in short, can be a great time- and work-saver, but procuring one is no small undertaking. Make your own assessment:

> **Doing your own housework** (with the family's help)
> *Loss:* Time, for all the things you'd rather be doing.
> *Gains:* Control over your environment (such as it is); healthful exercise; practical experience in manual labor for the kids; cash savings applicable to two weeks in the Caribbean.
> **Hiring it out**
> *Gains:* Free time for preferred activities; a cleaner house, possibly, than you'd manage on your own.
> *Losses:* A degree of privacy; a chunk of your income; your last excuse for ever having a messy house.

THE (PRACTICALLY) CAREFREE HOUSE

Whether you're doing your own housework or hiring it out, the same rule applies: The easier you can make it, the faster it'll get done. And when it comes to housework, the faster done the better.

Walls

An enamel paint, whether of matte or gloss finish, is much easier than flat paint to sponge-clean. *Latex* enamel is easiest to apply and the brushes and rollers can be cleaned with soap and water.

Vinyl wall paper, like enamel paint, is soil-resistant, and a well-chosen pattern will camouflage even the most persistent fingerprints. "Wallpaper tends to strengthen the wall, reinforcing it against gouges and scratches from toys or furniture," advises Beverly, an interior designer and mother of two. She also recommends burlap over fiberboard for a durable, economical wall covering.

Wood paneling, available in many grain finishes as well as tinted shades, never seems to get dirty. It simply grows more "earthy" looking as it darkens with age. Sponge it down occasionally and if you ever get tired of brown walls, paint over them.

Corkboard and *pegboard,* as described earlier, are not only functional but maintenance free.

Floors

Wall-to-wall carpeting has an enlarging, unifying effect in a small home or apartment. But avoid long shag varieties; they'll look matted and downtrodden moments after you're done vacuuming, and they'll soon show wear, especially under heavy traffic. Choose instead a short, tightly woven pile that is stain resistant. Nylon outlasts acrylic and other bargain synthetics. A light tweed, mottled, or heather tone is best. Remember, a dark, solid color is as quick to show cookie crumbs as white is to show spilled grape juice.

Natural oak flooring deserves to be shown off. Rent a floor sander to remove the old finish and scuff marks, then top the bare wood with two coats of polyurethane—a water-resistant, durable protective coating that comes in both high-gloss and satin finishes. Polyurethane can also be added over a floor that is stained or painted, but again, avoid a dark finish. It will display every footprint.

Wax-free linoleum is a popular choice for the kitchen, entryway, utility rooms, and other heavy-traffic areas. Most spills on linoleum clean up with a mild detergent and water, and when the built-in urethane finish dulls you can re-coat it to look like new again.

Quarry tile is another no-maintenance alternative for floors, imparting an austere elegance to any special room. It's expensive, but practically indestructible.

Windows

Curtains, unless you live in the Texas dustbowl, should need no more than a yearly washing or dry-cleaning. You'll probably get tired of them before they wear out, so choose whatever color and fabric appeals to you.

Vertical blinds, made of solid, hard vinyl, slide back and forth along a track. If one gets damaged, you replace it, not the whole set. These blinds need only an occasional wipe since, unlike traditional horizontal Venetian blinds, they catch very little dust.

Shades are a less expensive alternative to blinds, and accumulate little dirt—especially when they're rolled up. They can be laminated with paper or fabric to match your upholstery or wallpaper.

But if you live in an eighteenth-floor high-rise apartment or an isolated farmhouse overlooking a soybean field, why cover your windows with anything? Just enjoy the view!

Other Surfaces

Just as polyurethane protects your wood floors, it will safeguard the plant sill, kitchen table and chairs, and other rough-and-tumble furniture from spills and water rings.

Upholstery in vinyl may seem easy to wipe clean, but if it rips, it's done for. A thick, woven plaid or wide-wale corduroy, on the other hand, can be craftily mended in a manner that camouflages the tear. Look for a tag that says the fabric has been treated with Scotchgard or Zepel, or spray on a fabric protector yourself. It will be almost as spill-resistant.

It's practical to order extra arm covers for the sofa, and a square of carpet remnant to put by the front door, but don't leave the wrappers on the lamp shades or shroud your favorite furniture with a plastic throw. What are you preserving it for? A home should be enjoyed and lived in; whatever wears out in the course of normal use has served you well and can be fondly replaced.

Remember that your best bet for keeping dirt *off* is to keep it *out.* Place a scruffy thistle mat outside each entrance, and leave a box for muddy sneakers and boots. Keep your gardening shoes in the garage with the trowel, and hose the kids down when they come in from a hard day at the sandbox.

13

Soap, Soup, and Shopping

Years ago, an imaginative manufacturer came out with disposable party dresses. They were color-coordinated to match the paper napkins, tablecloths, and balloons used at parties, and featured adjustable fold-and-tear hemlines. But they turned out to be no threat to the garment industry. Besides being frumpy looking, the paper dresses answered no need. Laundering isn't such a big deal any more.

THE WASH CYCLE

It's not such a big deal, presuming you own your own washer and dryer. Otherwise you must imprison yourself in a laundromat, or sandwich-in only those errands that can be completed before the end of the rinse cycle. And unless you're cramming for an exam and can use the solitude of the laundromat productively, a home washer and dryer are indispensable timesavers. There is an automatic portable washer that hooks up to your kitchen sink and rolls conveniently out of the way when you're finished with it. The match-mate dryer, which vents out of the window, can be wall-mounted or stacked on top of the washer, on a special stand. And the apartment-sized compact clothes washer takes up no more space than an armchair.

And with your own machines, you can keep up with the wash on a daily basis, and not let it pile up like Mount Everest. It takes only a few spare moments to load the machine at night; run it when you get up the next morning; toss the wash in the dryer before you leave for work, and put it away when you get home.

Among all categories of housework, laundering offers the highest ratio of accomplishment to effort.

To eliminate the sorting process, use more than one clothes hamper. Assign one hamper for dark clothing like socks and jeans, one for light-colored items, and a third for permanent press items. Or have everyone put their light clothing (T-shirts, underwear) directly into the machine. When it's nearly full, toss in the towels and washcloths and run them through. Do other hamper-loads as necessary.

As the children get older, make each responsible for doing his or her own wash. This eliminates not only sorting but redistributing afterward.

Sock sorting is another tedious chore that is easily sidestepped:

- Buy only black or brown socks. Share them, in a community sock drawer, among all family members with similar-sized feet.
- Supply your family's sock-wearers with safety pins. Have them pin their socks together before washing, saving you from pairing them later.
- Buy extra pairs of socks for everyone, so that the supply doesn't run out so quickly.

Treat a stain as soon as you see it, instead of waiting to inspect every item before washing it. If you bleach clothing in a white porcelain sink, you'll brighten the sink along with the garments.

Some women recommend putting sheets right back on the bed after washing them, to save the time spent in folding and putting away. Do the same with towels—put them right back on the towel rack. I happen to think a change of color is worth the extra seconds of folding time, but the tip is worth sharing.

Washing-machine repairs can result from a sock or other small item flipping out of the tub during the spin cycle and getting stuck in the drainpipe. I learned this from a washing-machine repairman who, for forty-five dollars, extracted a sock from my drainpipe. To avoid this, load large items first, small items second, and medium-sized items on top, for ballast. Also, to get the best service from your machine, dissolve your detergent in water before adding the clothes (or use a liquid, pouring it directly onto the most soiled items), and clean your dryer-filter regularly.

Rinse out stockings and other hand-washables as you take a shower.

THE IRONING BORED

If ironing serves any useful purpose, it is probably to provide us with a guilt-free excuse for watching television. Wasting time at two things simultaneously somehow seems more constructive than wasting time at each, one after the other. You can also tell yourself that ironing helps develop good eye-hand coordination and is therapeutically relaxing.

I have tried all of these forms of rationalization, and have concluded that the best way to deal with ironing is to eliminate as much of it as possible:

- Send anything you're fussy about—large linen tablecloths, knife-pleated skirts, superstarched dress shirts, and the like—to a commercial laundry.
- Buy everything else possible in permanent press.

Permanent-press clothing must be rescued instantly at the end of the dryer cycle or it will wrinkle under its own weight. To avoid this inconvenience, don't use the dryer for polyester blends; instead, just hang them over the shower rod and let them drip dry overnight; transfer the hangers to the closet in the morning.

If you just couldn't resist that 100 percent cotton blouse (reminding yourself all the while that natural fibers do—really do—hold up best) dampen it before ironing with a spray from your plant vaporizer.

And switch on the 11 o'clock news.

FAST FOOD

Cooking is the part of housework many people enjoy most. Or at any rate, hate least. It's creative, whereas cleaning in its many forms is merely rehabilitative. And since we're past having to churn our own butter or draw water from the pump, it's not all that strenuous. In fact, after a hectic day of putting eight classes of junior-high physical education students through their paces, you may welcome a relaxed, mindless encounter with your Mouli grinder and wire wisk.

Ah, but after you've eaten, just when you should be savoring your accomplishment, you're faced with the cleanup. How ironic it is that the most "creative" aspect of housework also creates more drudgery. Make it easy on yourself by adhering to one unshakeable rule: *Clean as you go.* A good practice in any circumstance, it is indispensable in the kitchen.

For years the people I have lived with—parents, roommates, my husband—have urged this habit. "Put things away when you're done with them," they have nagged, "Don't leave them in the sink." But I had my own method, which was to take over the kitchen like Sherman's army crossing Georgia. Hauling out every available utensil and ingredient, I inched my way from one end of the counter to the next, leaving a trail of open bottles and eggshells. As the counters became too crowded to work on, I'd take over new territory—the space between the stove burners, the seat of a kitchen chair. Sometimes it took days to restore order after a major cooking orgy, or—more accurately—it took days to get motivated to do the job.

According to some logic, it might seem no harder to wash out four separate mixing bowls than to wash out the same bowl four times. But somehow, four bowls have an enervating effect. Just the sight of them seems to drain the spirit. Besides, they're all dry and crusty now, after sitting around for an hour, and will require soaking and scrubbing.

Here is another case in which slipping in something disagreeable—the cleaning—with something rewarding, the cooking, gets the disagreeable task painlessly over and done with.

So much for the cleanup. We will now proceed backwards, through the topics of freezing, fixing, and marketing.

A Freezer

A freezer can practically cut your cooking time in half, as you make it a habit to prepare multiple amounts of each recipe and freeze ahead meal-sized portions for later. What squirrelish satisfaction you'll derive from that stack of heat-and-serve dinners—all for the cost of one cooking session.

A twenty cubic-foot model is an asset, but you can get plenty of mileage from the freezer unit of your refrigerator. Organize it in three sections: Meats; fruits and vegetables; and breads and desserts. Invest in a dozen or more stackable pint- and quart-sized freezer containers, plastic bags with the twist ties, and some freezer-to-oven casserole dishes. Use a heavy plastic wrap or aluminum foil to cover the containers and dishes air-tight. Self-sticking labels, available at an office-supply store, are handy for marking and dating the containers' contents.

From now on, don't pass up specials on twenty-pound turkeys and rib roasts. Cook them up on the weekend, and freeze the additional servings sliced, diced, or in hunks, to accommodate various menu plans. (Do the same planning with fresh meats. Freeze your ground beef in patty form, for example, so that you're not hacking away at a solid ice-block of hamburger fifteen minutes before you'd hoped to serve dinner.)

Some good main dishes to prepare in quantity and freeze ahead include soups and stews, lasagna and other pasta dishes, stuffed green peppers or cabbage, meat loaf, meat balls, crepes, and baked or fried chicken. Don't hoard them for too long, though, for while fresh beef and poultry have a freezer life of up to a year, cooked meats and meat dishes will lose their flavor and texture after about ten weeks. Keep an inventory of the foods you have on hand and their storage expiration dates taped to the inside of a cupboard.

The freezer is also great for stockpiling those little extras that jazz up your dishes and desserts; for example:

- Chopped celery, peppers, and onions. Freeze them first on a cookie sheet so they won't stick together. (However, you'll have to use them for cooking; they won't be crisp enough for salads.)
- Grated cheese, crumbled cooked bacon, and cooked ground beef or sausage (add them to eggs, vegetables, or on top of a pizza).
- Chopped nuts, shaved chocolate, grated lemon or orange rind, or fresh coconut.
- Soup stock, to flavor gravies and sauces. Boil it down to a concentrate and freeze this in ice cube trays.
- Stale (but not moldy) bread. Save it for French toast, stuffings, croutons, or crumb toppings.

Other handy provisions, especially for unexpected company, include cookie dough (shaped like a sausage, ready to slice); quick breads and pound cake; bread and pizza dough; and pie crusts. Buy a package of reusable pie tins and the next time you feel in a mood for baking, roll out some extra dough, line the pans, and nest them in the freezer. You'll have a head start on a hearty meat pie, quiche, or favorite dessert.

Of course ready-made pie crusts, stuffed peppers, and the rest are also available in the frozen-foods section of your supermarket. Take advantage of this; there is no ancient rite of womanhood that says "Thou must make everything from scratch." Ready-made foods won't win you the Julia Child creative cooking award, but they will stave off hunger and cut preparation time to a minimum. Their disadvantage, along with high cost and sometimes questionable chemical additives, is their all-too-reliable taste. Each can of creamed soup tastes like the last of that brand, factory guaranteed. So use commercially canned, boxed, and frozen foods when it is expedient, but doctor them up a bit. Try some fresh curry seasoning, a bit of wine, or a topping of herb-flavored croutons and melted cheese.

Make Your Own Convenience Foods

This will save money and time. For a potent seasoned salt that is tasty in meat and poultry dishes or when sprinkled on eggs and vegetables, try:

Seasoned Salt

½ Cup salt
3   Tablespoons pepper
1   Tablespoons each: Garlic powder, onion powder
1   Teaspoon each: Sage, oregano, marjoram, rosemary, thyme, white pepper, nutmeg, celery seed

This is good on vegetables and salads:

Seasoned Salt II

2   Tablespoons seasoned salt (above)
2   Tablespoons parsley flakes
1   Tablespoon each: Dried lemon rind, basil, dried chives, dillweed, sesame seeds

Experiment with combinations of your favorite herbs and spices and concoct your own mixes for the kinds of foods you prepare often. A chili seasoning mix might combine seasoned salt, chili powder, cumin, garlic and oregano. Apple pie spice would combine cinnamon with a touch of nutmeg, coriander, ginger, allspice, and cloves.

The following biscuit mix can be stored in an air-tight canister and used for shortcakes, pancakes, pizza dough, and muffins.

Biscuit Mix

8 Cups flour
1½ Cups nonfat dry-milk powder
5 Tablespoons double-acting baking powder
1 Tablespoon salt
1 Cup butter, margarine, or white vegetable shortening

Mix the dry ingredients together in a large bowl. Cut in shortening until the mixture is very fine. This makes about eleven cups.

Basic Biscuits

Mix 2 cups of biscuit mix with about ½ cup of cold water. For shaped biscuits, pat soft dough to ½-inch thickness on a lightly floured board, cut in 2-inch circles, and place on a greased cookie sheet. For drop biscuits, add a tablespoon or two more of water to the mix and drop it from spoon. Bake in a preheated 425° oven for 10 to 12 minutes or until golden brown. Makes about 12.

Vary these biscuit recipes by adding a teaspoon of mixed herbs; or by sprinkling on grated Parmesan or cheddar cheese, cinnamon and sugar, or crumbled cooked bacon.

Shortcake, Coffeecake, or Muffins

Stir together:
2 Cups biscuit mix
⅓ Cup sugar
1 Large egg
½ Cup water or milk

Pour into a greased 9-inch cake pan or 12 lined muffin tins. Bake at 400° for 20 to 25 minutes (cake) or for 12 to 15 minutes (muffins).

Pancakes

Stir together:
2   Cups biscuit mix
2   Eggs
1   Cup water or milk
1   Tablespoon cooking oil

Pour about ¼ cup of batter on a hot griddle. Makes about 12 pancakes.

Pizza Dough

Mix together:
1   Package of yeast, softened in
½   Cup lukewarm water
2   Cups biscuit mix

Knead lightly and spread thinly over two, oiled 10-inch pizza pans or one 11-by-16-inch cookie sheet. You can allow this to rise for an hour for a thick, breadlike crust. But for a thinner crust in a hurry, top with tomato sauce, sausage, and cheese, and bake it immediately at 425° for 8 to 10 minutes.

Kitchen Equipment

Invest in appliances that save you cooking and preparation time—notably microwave ovens, food processors, pressure cookers, and crockpots. Choose cookware with a nonstick surface. Cookware of this type lacks the gourmet image (and cost) of heavy-duty aluminum and copper, but the speed of cleanup it gives you is worth more than snob appeal.

As for grinders, graters, and other gadgets, each is designed to save time, and you should therefore collect as many as you have use for and space for storing. For me, the essential items are sharp knives—paring, bread, tomato, and a meat cleaver (the latter, too lethal for public display, hangs behind a philodendron); a vegetable peeler; a hand mixer; three sizes of graters; measuring cups and spoons; a colander; a chopping block; and a heavy-duty can-opener that doesn't lose its grip halfway around the can. These rate top drawer or hanging space. Lower drawers are filled with useful but less fundamental items, such as a pizza-dough roller and a garlic press.

Menu Planning

It saves time to make large quantities of one or two dishes and carry them over to the next day. For example, if on Sunday you serve roast beef, baked potatoes, and mixed vegetables, on Monday you can serve beef stew, cole slaw, and freshly baked bread. On Tuesday, the stew, with the addition of tomato or V-8 juice, becomes soup, and the bread makes open-faced sandwiches. Designate one area of the refrigerator—perhaps a turntable or slide-out tray—for leftovers, and check it daily to see what can be incorporated into the next meal.

Family meals can become rather repetitious especially if you're cooking for people whose tastes are limited. Nothing is more frustrating than to commit an afternoon to assembling a splendid Gratin de Morue (cod casserole) and be greeted with a shrill and indignant "What's *this*? I don't like it!" This is particularly unnerving if the shrill voice is that of your husband.

You can respond in one of three ways:

1. Dump the plate over the complainer's head.
2. Capitulate, and serve nothing but hot dogs and spaghetti.
3. Involve the whole family in meal planning, securing their promise to *try everything*. Team an experimental recipe such as ham croquettes with an equally nutritious, tried-and-true side dish such as deviled eggs so that no one goes hungry.

"I have a super system for organizing meals and grocery shopping," says Nancy, a California textile artist. "I keep a card file, with each card listing a main dish with its recipe, ingredients, and suggestions of what to serve with it. Every week the dinners are chosen from this box by all four family members. Each gets to choose one or two meals, and in this way everyone is guaranteed that during the week they will get one or two dinners they *like*. Previously chosen cards go to the back of the box, so that we don't have meat loaf once a week simply because child number two loves it, and it is easy to make up a grocery list because the ingredients are listed on each card."

BRINGING HOME THE BACON

You can cut the time you spend grocery shopping to an hour per week—and eliminate those obnoxious emergency milk runs altogether—by developing a routine. Here's how:

Keep a centrally posted grocery list. On this list, each family member notes when a favorite food is running low and adds his or her own special requests. Add to this the ingredients needed for the week's menus and any staples that need restocking. Also, be sure to run a quick inventory of non-food necessities, such as soap powders and paper products, and add them to the list as needed.

If you clip coupons (the savings are worth the effort, providing you stick with items you'd be buying anyway) take along those that relate to your grocery list or are near expiration. I write my list on the back of a business envelope and tuck the coupons inside. Inexpensive, purse-sized coupon organizers with indexed pockets are available now at most supermarkets.

Settle on one reliable well stocked supermarket. Do this rather than trying to shuttle back and forth from one store to the next in pursuit of bargains that may be sold out by the time you get there. Choose your store on the basis of proximity, prices, quality, and service (a key service being the number of cashiers available to assure a speedy checkout). Other conveniences to look for might include a delicatessen and a fresh-baked goods section, or a prescription service.

Learn the layout. Bonnie, mother of three teenagers, recommends making a chart of routinely used family staples and grouping them according to the supermarket aisle in which they're located. "It took me less than thirty minutes to make up such a list and mimeograph typed copies," she reports. "Checking off the foods that are needed is much easier than re-thinking each item."

Stick to your list. However, be flexible enough to make substitutions and take advantage of specials. Stockpile easy-to-prepare family favorites such as frozen pizza, macaroni and cheese, breakfast bars—anything that can supply sustenance in short order if a meal plan gets altered.

Shop when the store is least crowded. The cashier can advise you about this, letting you avoid especially the 5:30 to 7 P.M. rush hour and Saturday mornings. Obtain a check-cashing card from the store so that you don't have to wait for three assistant managers to approve your references. Or pay with cash.

Bag your own groceries. Group frozen foods in one bag, refrigerator foods in a second bag, pantry items in a third bag, and so on to save time in putting everything away.

Grocery shopping alone is at least 20 percent faster and 20 percent cheaper than shopping with the kids. ("Aw, Mom, just one bag of Cheetos?" "Just five boxes of Captain Crunch and I can send off for this space rocket!") If you must bring your children, make it quality time, an educational experience. Teach them about unit pricing, size comparisons, and testing for freshness. Let them help select and weigh the produce.

PACKAGING

From the well-stocked refrigerator we move on to the empty closet.

Not really empty, of course; it's just that you haven't a thing to wear. Just when you'd mastered the ethnic peasant look, everything turned to silk shirts and Harris tweeds.

While shopping for a blazer is not quite like shopping for broccoli, many of the same principles apply. You take inventory of what you have, decide what you need, shop strategically and purposefully, and stick with one or two good stores, not the whole shopping mall.

What you wear is important because, fairly or not, some people are going to judge your competence by your appearance. Your clothes may announce that you are imaginative and self-confident or that you're ineffectual and careless. It's not that people mean to treat you superficially; they just don't have time to hear your credentials.

Saunter into a business meeting in an outfit that is too casual, provocative, or otherwise inappropriate and you may leave the impression that you don't take seriously your job or the people you're meeting with. On the other hand, clothes that are polished and professional looking subtly imply that you know what you're doing.

A professional image saves you time because it eliminates having to prove yourself.

It wasn't until the late seventies that designers began to notice the needs of working women; an Associated Merchandising Corporation study described the market as one of "untapped and unexplored potential," predicting that by 1981, working women would account for $128 billion in earnings and $12 billion spent on work-related apparel. More important, said the report, women would be willing to spend a little extra for quality and durability.[1]

To assemble this attractive, versatile, image-boosting wardrobe without taking out a second mortgage, note that parts of it are probably already hanging in your closet. Begin by assessing what you have already. "Separate your wardrobe into two categories, the winners and the mistakes,"[2] suggests Lila Nadell, syndicated fashion columnist.

The mistakes are those things you never seem to get around to wearing—the fuschia pants that were such a bargain at half price; the cowl-neck sweater from your mother that makes you look like a furry turtle. Give them all to the church relief fund, or to your sister who's making a quilt. My rule of thumb is, if it hasn't been worn in a year, out it goes. Why leave these items to take up drawer space, as monuments to bygone styles and poor judgement?

With the mistakes cheerfully disposed of, you can appraise the winners in your wardrobe. Separate them into color families, suggests Lila Nadell, such as all the browns and all the blues. Within each color group, see how the jackets, pants, skirts, and other garments can be mixed and matched. What new color combinations are possible? This kind of analyzing and sorting can help you spot gaps in your wardrobe so that you can make informed choices on your next shopping trip.

Once you've determined that white wool pants and a navy blue suit will pull together the look you want, "shop the market." Like a professional buyer for a fashion chain, make an exploratory trip through various stores and departments to see what is available in various styles and price ranges. Cover as much territory as you have time for, from the largest department and discount stores to the back-alley boutiques.

Repeat this review process each spring and fall, and fill the gaps in your wardrobe early, when the selection is best. You may get more mile-

[1] Bridget O'Brian, "Looking the Part," *Working Woman,* June 1979, pp. 26-27.
[2] Lila Nadell, "How to Be a Better Shopper than You've Ever Been Before," courtesy *Glamour,* April 1979, p. 331. Copyright© 1979 by The Condé Nast Publications, Inc.

age out of something "perfect" chosen at full price than from a half-dozen compromises taken from the clearance rack.

"When I was a student I only shopped the sales," relates Kathie, a sales-management trainee. "It was a game I played to convince myself I was a shrewd bargain hunter. If I saw a designer dress reduced by half, I'd lose all perspective about how it looked on me or whether I needed it in the first place. And if someone paid me a compliment, I could always win extra praise by responding triumphantly, 'I got it on sale!'

"When it became time to go on job interviews, however," she continues, "I saw that what I owned was a closet full of separates that hardly matched anything except white blouses or black skirts. There were even a few things I'd never worn because, consistent with their low price, they never fit right."

With a demanding new job and new priorities, Kathie has cut her leisure-time shopping forays from several per week to several per year. She now looks for one or two "really nice, versatile outfits, buying the coordinating jacket, shirt, and accessories at once instead of adding them piecemeal throughout the year. It seems like a big outlay of money in one shot, but actually I'm keeping within the same budget as before. When you pick clothes for their looks instead of their price, you don't tire of them so quickly."

Kathie and several other women I surveyed also recommend catalogue shopping—for everything from mundane necessities such as underwear and bed linens to classic clothes and exotic gifts. In most cases you can just telephone your order and have it charged or sent C.O.D. The two- to five-dollar delivery charge is fair exchange for the savings in time, gas, and parking. When buying gifts, have them wrapped and delivered directly to the recipient, to save two separate mailings.

When you do prefer to shop live and in person, the following strategies will speed things up a bit:

- Limit yourself to one or two stores which offer you the best quality and selection within your price range, as well as parking convenience and a no-hassle return policy. Learn which of the brands there fit you best. Get to know one of the salespersons and ask her or him to watch for certain items and hold them in your size.

- Investigate some of the "corporate careers" shops opening in more and more large department stores. These special boutiques are geared to pulling together a professional look, from blouse to briefcase, for the busy working woman. Many employ personal shoppers to assist in your initial choices, keep them on file, and suggest future choices.
- A store credit card will save you time both in making purchases and with returns. Cash is fine, but checks take the longest time to clear, often having to be cross-referenced against three pieces of I.D. and approved by a supervisor who is probably on coffee break.
- Shop when the stores are least crowded. This is almost always before 11:30 A.M., between 2 and 4 P.M., and after 7:30 P.M. Avoid the lunch hour and late afternoon, when the stores fill with purchasers on their way home from work. Especially avoid the weekends before and after Christmas. Weekdays, except for Saturday mornings, are less crowded than weekends; if you come early, you'll have a full sales staff and a nearly empty store, all to yourself.
- If you're looking for something to match a specific outfit, wear the outfit or bring it with you. Even as common a shade as navy varies from royal blue to almost black. Also bring the shoes you plan to wear with the outfit, so that you can judge the total effect.
- Try to hold out for something you really like; don't just buy for the sake of buying. If it really bugs you to waste an afternoon looking and coming home empty-handed, call it research.
- Keep all sales slips. It's hard to return something without one, even if it has an obvious defect. Designate a drawer or shoebox for all receipts and keep them for at least six months. One woman I know got a pair of sandals replaced after arguing successfully that at forty dollars they should have lasted more than one summer!
- Shop for birthday, anniversary, and holiday gifts all year long—don't wait until the eve of the special occasion itself. Some of the most original and often economical gifts are to be found at summer art fairs, antique shows, and seasonal clearance sales. Make a habit of buying "the perfect present" when you see it, and save yourself a frustrating search in the future.

(14)

Time Out

Up at 6 A.M. Wash the floors, walls, and windows; vacuum the upholstery and drapes. Starch and iron the table linens; polish the silver. Bone and marinate the chicken breasts; boil the bones for a soup base; assemble the stuffed grape leaves and seven-layer chocolate torte. Rush the dress to the dry-cleaners, locate stockings without runs, and deliberate twenty minutes between a pearl necklace and an enameled pendant.

This is only the day *before* the party. By the time the guests appear tomorrow, the hostess will be numb with exhaustion.

The occasion is not a banquet for fifty heads-of-state—just two neighborhood couples over for dinner.

A wild exaggeration? Unfortunately, this scenario seems to be a common phase many young women go through as fledgling hostesses. We want to make a good impression. We want everyone to have a good time, but we aren't sure how to guarantee it. So we fall back on the notion—tried but untrue—that enormous effort assures dazzling success.

Some people equate giving a party to staging a theatrical production. They plan every detail—props, lighting, special effects. Even a bridge foursome is a major undertaking, right down to the color coordination of the tablecloth and tally sheets.

Such people set standards of entertaining that are difficult to meet and impossible to sustain. Inevitably, after having a baby, getting a new job, going back to school, or taking on other new commitments, these women move social life to the bottom of their priorities. Unable to justify the *preparation* time they think is required, they stop inviting anybody over to do anything.

117

"Since I went back to work, I see very little of my old friends," sighs Sally, a public health nurse. "I'm on my feet all day talking to physicians and patients, so on weekends I mainly curl up with a good book. When I'm not too tired, I feel I should be doing something constructive, like catching up with the housework.

"Still," she adds wistfully, "I miss having conversations on subjects other than blood clots."

CELEBRATE!

Is this you, always too busy or too tired to spend time with good friends? Then what is the point of all this hard work? With whom will you share its rewards, your success? All work and no play, which makes Jack a dull boy, does nothing for Jill's personality either!

The theme of this chapter is play without work. Entertaining should be as enjoyable and effortless for you as it is for your guests. Is that asking too much? Not if you keep your priorities intact.

The purpose of a social gathering is to celebrate and perpetuate friendship. Your friends are coming over to see you (and each other), not to critique your Béarnaise sauce or check for mildew behind the shower curtain. Your only objective is to encourage them to have a good time and to enjoy their company.

In this relaxed frame of mind you can go about your preparations in an organized, rational manner, knowing that the only person you really have to please is yourself. Clean to the point that it satisfies you, not to some mythical standard imposed by a TV commercial. Don't think about the drudgery of extra cleaning but about how nice the place will still look the next day, when you can quietly relax and enjoy it.

Concentrate on surfaces: Vacuum the floor, sponge off the table tops, make sure the bathroom's clean. But don't overkill. There's no need to mop behind the refrigerator unless you're planning to seat people there. Furthermore,

- You don't need to take on the whole house, from basement to attic. Just close off the bedrooms and other areas that won't be in use; or
- Close off the whole house and hold a backyard barbecue. If there isn't time to mow the lawn...

• Remove the event from your property altogether and head for a nearby park for a picnic.

LIGHT REFRESHMENTS

If you love to cook, you probably look forward to social gatherings as an excuse for experimenting with new recipes and showing off your skills. Cooking can be a very satisfying creative outlet if you don't put yourself under needless pressure by: (1) doing too much; or (2) waiting until the last minute; or both.

Don't insist on cooking everything from scratch. A package of frozen egg-roll wrappers can save you an hour of tedious dough stretching; canned broth is almost indistinguishable from bones that have simmered since sunup.

Do prepare everything in advance.

• A week or more ahead of time you can fix and freeze festive main dishes, such as lasagna or stuffed crepes; vegetable casseroles; partially baked breads or dinner rolls; cakes, fruit pies, and empty pastry shells.
• A day or two ahead you can make molded salads, sauces, and dips; prepare any dishes that need to be aged, such as marinated meats or vegetables, cheese balls, or brandied desserts; and make extra ice cubes.
• The morning of the event, if you must market for fresh foods, work from a list. That way you won't forget any minute essentials, such as seasonings or garnishes. Prepare salad or raw vegetables for crudités, rinsing and wrapping them air-tight so that they will stay crisp. Cut fruit can be sprinkled with lemon juice to prevent it from turning brown. Bread and rolls, wrapped in aluminum foil, are ready for warming. Arrange all dishes in the refrigerator so that they are accessible in the order that they will be popped into the oven or put on the table.

If you don't like to cook, there are two simple alternatives: Do as little cooking as possible, or don't do it at all.

• People simply won't bear a grudge against you for serving ready-made guacamolé dip or opening a canned ham. Take full advantage of pre-packaged mixes and sauces, and never apologize for being expedient.

- Plan the whole menu from foods that are sold ready-to-serve. The delicatessen can supply everything from roast beef and cold cuts to chutney and chopped liver. Buy an assortment of bakery goodies for dessert.
- Let your guests put their own meal together. For example, set up a salad bar with the basic greens and raw vegetables, grated cheese, crumbled bacon, and maybe some bean sprouts and artichoke hearts. Use the same type of buffet spread for customized hero sandwiches. Line up an assortment of ice creams, liqueurs, cut fruits, toasted nuts, and other toppings for sundae desserts.
- Let your guests cook the whole meal, start to finish. You provide the raw ingredients, recipes, tools, and work space; they do the rest. This is a great way to introduce complicated ethnic dishes. One hostess, a relentless matchmaker, has also found it an excellent way to pair off her single friends.
- Share the work, share the glory. That's the rationale behind progressive dinners and pot-luck parties. Each person or couple contributes one dish in large quantity. You supply just enough coordination to prevent the appearance of five macaroni salads.
- If nobody feels like cooking, let the professionals take charge. Hire a caterer. Reserve a table at an elegant restaurant. Order chop suey to go. Send out for pizza.

Here are some general suggestions to minimize the time and stress involved in any form of entertaining, large-scale or small.

- Get everything ready in advance except for ladling up the meat and vegetables. Always have the table set, the coasters out, the wine ready to pour. Such preparation conveys a tone of caring ("look at the trouble she went to for us") and welcome. It also frees you to relax and enjoy the company of your guests.
- Keep the menu simple. Judy, a Baltimore hostess, recommends including just one special, unusual dish per meal. It will stand out more among the rest of the fare, and will keep your cooking less complicated.
- To make sure everything is ready ahead of time, set deadlines. "By noon I'll have the canapés chilling in the refrigerator; by five the house will be straight and vacuumed so that I can take a leisurely bath."
- Invite people at least a week ahead of time so that *they* can plan ahead and adjust their schedules. Save them further time and confusion by being specific. Don't say, "Wear whatever you feel like" if you'll be in black chiffon. Don't say, "Anytime after work" if you mean 6 P.M.

- Involve your children. Older children can pass drinks and appetizers, empty ashtrays, help serve, or clear the table. Younger ones can answer the door and collect coats. Some parents pay their kids for such services, but many kids feel that being included in the festivities and sharing a few nibbles of fancy food is reward in itself.
- If you have an infant or a rowdy toddler to contend with, consider hiring a babysitter to keep the child occupied until bedtime. You do this routinely when you're going out for the evening; give yourself the same break some night when you're staying in.
- Invite people with mutual interests and complementary personalities. Balance listeners with talkers, shy people with extroverts. If you're inviting some new acquaintances, include some old friends with whom you feel relaxed and comfortable. In short, by assembling a group that can generate its own conversation, you relieve yourself of the burden of "keeping the party going."
- Food needn't be the central theme of a get-together. Plan a gathering around an evening at the theater or an afternoon sports event. Invite people over to watch a television special, or pool their slides from summer vacation for a group show-and-tell. Get a crew together for volleyball, skating, dancing, or Monopoly.

These events cost you little in time or effort. You're merely the instigator. The entertainment takes care of itself.

GEE, THIS HAS BEEN FUN

Finally, what do you do when the event has been so successful that you're dead on your feet and a few stragglers show no signs of leaving? Short of yawning demonstrably and shaking your wristwatch, there are some tactful ways to cue your guests that the party's over.

One hostess suggests making a comment like, "It sure has been good seeing you again. We should get together more often." By focusing on a future event, she conveys the idea that this one has ended.

An offer of more food and coffee presents a choice of either leaving now or lingering twenty more minutes. An astute guest usually picks the first alternative.

A third, less subtle method is to begin collecting empty cups and ashtrays and stacking them in the kitchen. If this doesn't work, begin washing them.

In the end, there is no substitute for friendly directness. "I hate to be a spoilsport but I'm too tired to carry on a coherent conversation and I have to be up early tomorrow." People will appreciate—and probably reciprocate—your honesty.

Even in a social situation, straightforward communication saves guesswork. And that saves time for everybody.

15
The Energy Crisis

Doing your best takes feeling your best. None of the information in this book will be of much use to you if you are perpetually exhausted.

Compare your body to a car. (A sporty little TR-7?...a nice sturdy Volvo?) Whatever your self-image, you can improve it with preventive maintenance. For top performance and mileage you need to use quality fuel, get regular tune-ups, and rev up the engine occasionally.

You already know what's good for you. Ever since childhood you've been exhorted to get plenty of fresh air and exercise; finish your vegetables; get your beauty sleep. But these things take time, and to gain time you drive instead of walk, grab a chocolate bar in place of lunch, work until the wee hours of morning, and put off seeing the doctor until you think you're pregnant.

The issue is not *why* you should take excellent care of yourself but *how* to do it on a jam-packed schedule.

FUEL

Overfed, overweight, and undernourished—many of us eat to prevent hunger rather than to alleviate it. Or we eat to pick up our spir-

its, be sociable, or relieve boredom. Food as entertainment is more likely to be a fudge brownie than a celery stick.

Besides, mealtime always seems to be the rush hour.

Francine sees to it that her children have eggs, juice, and milk in
the morning before she hurries off to work; for her it's coffee and a
danish from the office vending machine. She skips lunch to run a few
errands, stopping last for a can of Pepsi and a package of cheese crackers to eat at her desk. Famished when she arrives home, she gobbles up
handfuls of layer cake while preparing dinner. By the time it's ready,
she's no longer hungry.

Eating habits like these leave you feeling bloated and slug-
gish—hardly a state that's conducive to peak performance. And those
surplus starches and sweets will collect about your hips, further sapping
your energy and self-confidence.

If you've been "meaning to go on a diet," now is the time. You're
shaping up your house, your job, your life,...why not yourself? Bone
up on nutritional and caloric values and resolve that from now on, the
foods you eat are going to work for your body, not just take up space.

Sensible eating calls for a whole new definition of "fast food." A
Big Mac, fries, and a strawberry shake cost close to 1,000 calories while
supplying only a fraction of the day's needed protein and nutrients.
You can substitute the following in less time than it takes to stand in line
under the golden arches:

Breakfast: Concoct a high-protein milkshake in the blender, with
a banana and skim milk. For variations, add wheat germ, a raw egg, or-
ange-juice concentrate, or malted-milk mix. Hard-boil some eggs, slice
them on whole-wheat toast, top with cheese, and put the open-faced
sandwich in the toaster oven for a minute until the cheese melts. Jazz up
a cooked cereal with sliced fruit, raisins, or nuts. Bring a slice of whole-
grain bread and fruit to the office for a midmorning coffee break.

Lunch: Bringing your own saves time and money, and you retain
quality control. Pack a small plastic container with raw vegetables and
fruit; cottage cheese mixed with chives; cold baked chicken; yogurt; celery stuffed with cream cheese, peanut butter, or tuna salad; stuffed pita
bread; or cheese and crackers. Make and freeze a week's worth of sandwiches on Sunday night (and have all lunch packers in the family do
likewise). If you do choose to have lunch at a restaurant, pick one that
requires at least a four-block walk and has a salad bar.

Dinner: Keep a supply of prepared-in-advance frozen main dishes. (For ideas, see Chapter 13.) Add side dishes that require no fussing, such as cottage cheese, canned vegetables, or rice. Make a big tossed, marinated, or molded salad that can see you through several meals. Keep desserts simple too, such as ice cream or fruit.

Tally up the day's calorie consumption before dinner, and if you find that you blew your limit at Swen's Smorgasbord at noon, excuse yourself now. If you must make a meal for the rest of the family, fix them something you dislike so you're not even tempted.

Snacks: Strip your cupboards and refrigerator of cookies, chips, curls, puffs, and all the other nutritionally empty crunchies you find irresistible. Substitute a carton of crisp carrot and celery sticks, mushrooms, cauliflower, or zucchini strips. Make a dip from yogurt (not sour cream) and dried onion soup. Make a batch of popcorn and sprinkle it with parmesan cheese. Substitute iced tea or mineral water for soda pop; and dry wine for high-calorie beer, mixed drinks, or straight liquor. There's nothing unsound about snacking, so long as you choose healthful foods and keep track of them. It doesn't matter when you eat, or how much at a time, but what it all adds up to.

SUPER OCTANE

Some foods are rumored to do more than simply sustain the life processes. Impressive claims of higher stamina, greater longevity, and increased sexual prowess have been made for a wide range of substances from Geritol to ginseng tea. Do certain tonics and "health foods" have magical properties that will enable you to leap tall buildings and bend steel with your bare hands? You'll get a much different answer from a nutritionist than from a granola merchant.

"High-energy food" is really a euphemism for high-calorie food. And a calorie is a calorie, whether it resides in a carrot or a cream puff. A unit of heat measurement, one calorie is equivalent to the amount of energy required to raise the temperature of a gram of water by one degree centigrade. Like an engine, the body converts the caloric energy of food into fuel for growth, movement, and other bodily functions.

The "high-energy" dried fruits, nuts, and sunflower seeds touted by health-food faddists are great sources of magnesium and potassium but, gram for gram, they are also great sources of calories; a half-cup of dry-roasted peanuts—a mere couple of handfuls—contains over 400 calories! They're good for you. But if your intake exceeds your physical activity output, those high-protein peanuts will be stored as fat, the same way that potato chips will.

"Frankly, more of us are urging the populous to decrease the ratio of calories to food weight," says Dr. Stanley M. Garn, professor of human nutrition and anthropology, and fellow of the University of Michigan Center for Human Growth and Development. "Salads, fruits, and nice chewy bread are foods with fewer calories per density. Their bulk evens out absorption and prevents peaks in blood sugars."

Candy, sugar and honey are sometimes portrayed as "quick-energy sources." That's because it takes less time for your body to convert them into glucose, the body's fuel. The rise in blood sugar alleviates hunger, but the effect is only temporary. And the "lift" you seem to feel is probably psychological, attributable to that yummy chocolate-and-caramel taste. Furthermore, the glucose you don't burn off is stored as fat. Totally lacking in nutrients, sugar is more apt to put inches around your waist than to put a firecracker under your heels.

Coffee may seem to get your juices flowing in the morning, but the source of the stimulation is caffeine. And too much caffeine will make you jumpy, not energetic. Some people find that coffee or tea keeps them awake at night; then they gulp down more the next morning to mask their fatigue. Laden with sugar and cream, coffee can also add hundreds of near-empty calories to your diet. When coffee begins to make you feel agitated instead of refreshed, it's time to switch to a decaffeinated brand, or to limit your consumption.

As for vitamins, most doctors agree that a person who eats a varied and well-balanced diet needs no vitamin supplements. "Taking a multivitamin tablet as 'insurance' occasionally, when you think you've fallen below your RDA (recommended daily allowance), is good for the vitamin industry but no better for you," advises Stanley Garn, noting that "the American Academy of Pediatrics does not recommend vitamin supplements for children."

Megavitamins—massive doses of vitamins A, B, C, and the rest of the "alphabet" vitamins—are not only "not recommended" by doctors and nutritionists, they are vigorously discouraged. Vitamin faddists figure that if five milligrams of something is good for you, 500 milligrams must be a hundred times better. Not true, say most medical authorities. The excess is simply excreted by the system. You may as well pour them down the drain. And in the case of vitamins A and D, which are fat-soluble and kept by the body in fatty, adipose tissue, the overdose may be dangerous.

Nationally prominent nutritionist Dr. Jean Mayer stresses that too little is known about the long-term effects of megavitamins. "Large doses much in excess of the established daily allowances are needed only in certain disease states and should be taken only by prescription of a physician. In normal amounts, vitamins are food; at five, ten, a hundred or a thousand times the normal level, vitamins are drugs and should be treated accordingly."[1]

Do You Have "Tired Blood?"

The television commercials imply that iron supplements will make women feel younger, peppier and more loved. Consumers Union says that, for most women, iron supplements are a waste of money. You can get an adequate supply, they state, from such sources as meats (especially liver), fish, dried fruits, whole wheat, beans, and green, leafy vegetables.[2] Your doctor may recommend an iron supplement in cases of pregnancy or excessive menstruation. But that phrase bantered about by TV announcers—"iron deficiency anemia"—is difficult to self-diagnose. If you experience heart palpitations, breathing problems, or chronic fatigue, see your doctor, not your druggist.

The consensus among medical authorities seems to be that special foods, pills, and other reputed energy potions are superfluous at best. They can even be detrimental, both to your body and to your budget. Instead, aim for variation in what you eat. Try different brands, different restaurants, and the widest possible variety of fresh fruits and vegetables, whole grains, and animal and dairy products. The odds are that you'll cover all nutritional bases.

[1]Dr. Jean Mayer, *A Diet for Living* (New York: David McKay Co., Inc., 1975), p. 49.

[2]Copyright 1978 by Consumers Union of United States, Inc., Mount Vernon, N.Y. 10550. Excerpted by permission from *Consumer Reports*, September 1978.

CAUTION, CONTENTS UNDER PRESSURE

Diet is only one of a number of factors that can affect your energy level. If you feel tired day after day, it probably has less to do with what you're eating than with what's eating you.

Dissatisfaction with work, pressures from school, a whopping argument with someone you love—even a dreary day in February can leave you listless and unmotivated. Often the emotional stress of a situation is far more taxing than any physical effort.

"I can't understand why I'm so tired every evening," sighs Lydia, an airline reservations clerk. "I'm sitting all day, either talking on the phone or typing into a computer. What can be hard about that?"

What she doesn't stop to think about is the pressure that builds from dealing with impatient customers and a demanding supervisor who monitors the time it takes her to handle requests.

Stress can occur in any job, custodial through executive. It has been widely reported that as women gain more prestigious and powerful jobs in the corporate hierarchy, they become more susceptible to heart attacks, high blood pressure, stomach disorders, and other stress-related illnesses. Housewives, on the other hand, may experience frustration and fatigue for an opposite reason—because their job isn't challenging enough.

Finally, stress can result from trying to combine many roles. Here you are, getting the kids up and off to school or to the sitter, yourself off to work, the bills paid, the house kept up, and you feel pretty competent. But it's like cycling across a high-wire while juggling flaming torches. A momentary loss of balance (the car doesn't start, the baby is running a fever) and your whole act goes tumbling to the ground in defeat.

A certain degree of tension is good for you. It gets the old adrenalin going and keeps you feeling alert and motivated. But too much has the reverse effect. It drains your psychic energy, producing a state of chronic fatigue.

The source of the problem doesn't seem to be an overload of responsibility but a loss of control.

"I love being a teacher and I'm good at it," states Janice, who has spent eleven years with a large suburban school system. "But the new principal and I don't seem to communicate. He has challenged my teaching methods and insisted on new curriculum materials. Now he is interfering with my handling of student discipline problems. I can't afford to lose my seniority here, yet I dread going to work every day for fear of another confrontation. Let him run the school and give *me* control over the decisions that affect my competence as a teacher!''

There are a number of ways to alleviate stress (see "Anxiety," Chapter 3) but first you must:

- Identify the source. If it's a person, confront him or her and attempt to settle your differences. Clarify expectations, theirs and yours, so you can stop worrying whether you're doing the right things or leaving yourself open to more criticism.
- If it's a situation that has you under pressure either at home or at work, take immediate action to bring it under control. If it is currently beyond your control, it may still help to discuss it with someone whose judgement you trust. Worries tend to grow when you bottle them up. Give them air. This will help you to...
- Get your mind on other things. If the stress has to do with your job, don't haul it home in your briefcase. If the source of the stress is at home, break away for a period of time and do something diverting and self-indulgent. Pursue a hobby, one in which you can lose yourself. Plan a vacation or at least a long weekend. But don't take off while the pressure's on. Resolve the conflict, and then reward yourself.

LIMBERING UP

One of the best ways to achieve that needed change of pace, relieve tension and fatigue, tone your muscles, and feel simply terrific is exercise. If this conjures up memories of thirty sit-ups to the shrill beat of the gym teacher's whistle, and laps around the high-school football field, you're in for a pleasant surprise. Exercise needn't be boring or torturous. And like petty cash, wisely invested, it actually creates energy even as you're expending it.

Here's how. Aerobic exercise, the kind you get from at least twenty minutes of vigorous swimming, jogging, rope skipping—or anything that makes you huff and puff a bit—increases the number and size of your red-blood vessels and creates more oxygen-carrying red blood cells. It strengthens your heart, improves your lung capacity, and lowers your pulse rate. As a result, you can work harder and play longer. You have more stamina.

A program of sustained aerobic exercise on at least three nonconsecutive days per week, plus a well-rounded regular routine of limbering up, muscle stretching, and strengthening exercises, will help you control your weight, firm up your figure, clear your complexion, and improve all your bodily functions. You'll not only sleep better, but you'll probably require less sleep. This alone may gain you several extra hours of free time per week.

Fitness, in short, gives you an energy reserve for doing more of the things you enjoy, whether it's working, dancing, or partying with friends. It will also give you the added endurance to withstand mental or physical stress, plus an overall sense of well-being (that "healthy glow") that comes with feeling good about yourself.

At Purdue University, physical education Professor A. H. Ismail studied the psychological effects of regular exercise on a group of previously sedentary staff members, aged thirty-five to fifty-five years. Personality tests conducted at the beginning and end of the program showed that the exercisers were "more confident, imaginative and self-sufficient" than they had been at the beginning of the project, and considerably better in these psychological measures than their inactive counterparts. "Not only are people who are in good physical condition better physiologically, they are superior emotionally," Ismail concluded. "Physical and emotional health go hand in hand."

Supporting this are dozens of personal testimonies from my surveys.

"I used to drag myself home after work, cook dinner for the kids, plop down with the newspaper, and hardly be able to move until bedtime," relates Mary, a social worker. "I was thirty-four years old and I felt like seventy. Then one especially hot summer I began going for a swim on the way home from work. I began doing laps, trying to increase my quota a little each week. To my amazement, I finished these sessions feeling lots more energetic and refreshed than when I began. I felt guilty at first about getting home an hour later, but my kids, noticing my improved disposition, said they didn't mind a bit. Sometimes they have supper waiting for me."

In a Philadelphia law office, a group of women who used to meet for lunch at a downtown cafeteria now head for the local fitness club. They run, swim, play racquetball, or use the exercise machines. One of them lifts weights. As a group they have lost about forty pounds, but what's far more impressive is what they say they've gained: A renewed self-image and outlook on their work and leisure pursuits. Says one, "We even enjoy a special kind of locker-room camaraderie—the kind that used to be confined to 'the male experience.'"

Such success stories are familiar, of course. But knowing the benefits of exercise isn't enough. You've got to experience it, and keep at it.

First, pick a sport that you really enjoy; one that is so reinforcing that it can rank among the joys of your life instead of the drudgeries. Would you prefer something solitary (jogging, skating, swimming) or social (tennis, team sports)? Perhaps something exotic like belly dancing or scuba diving would create a real change of pace.

Fit your activity into a time of the day that you tend to waste anyway. Maybe an early morning run will get the juices flowing, or an after work tennis date will revive your spirits. Find a time that works best for you, and then treat it as a standing appointment. Make it as regular a part of your daily routine as sleeping and eating.

Compete with yourself. Nobody says you have to be Dorothy Hamill or Chris Evert Lloyd or even your friend in the next apartment, who is nine years older than you and ten times as fast. It's saner to exercise at your own pace on a regular basis, and to chart your own progress.

One way to track your progress with aerobic exercise is by monitoring your pulse rate. To do this, using your first two fingers, press lightly along the thumb side of your wrist or at the angle formed where your neck meets your jaw. Count the number of beats you feel in ten seconds, multiply by six, and you'll have your *resting heart rate* per minute.

Now, subtract your age from 220 and you'll have your *maximum heart rate.* (Example, if you're thirty, the fastest your heart should beat without your passing out is 190 beats per minute.)

Determine your *heart-rate reserve* by subtracting your resting heart rate from your age-predicted maximum heart rate. (Example, if your resting heart rate is 70, your heart-rate reserve will be 120.)

For your *heart-rate training range,* multiply 0.6 and 0.8 times the heart-rate reserve and add the result to your resting heart rate. Your ideal training rate is one that surpasses the lower limit but not the upper one, and can eventually be sustained for at least thirty minutes.

> Example: Julie Smith, age thirty
> Resting pulse rate: 70 beats per minute
> Maximum heart rate: $220 - 30 = 190$ beats per minute
> Heart-rate reserve: $190 - 70 = 120$ beats per minute
> Heart-rate training range:

$$\begin{array}{cc} 120 & 120 \\ \times .6 & \times .8 \\ \hline 72 & 96 \\ +70 & +70 \\ \hline 142 \quad \text{to} & 166 \text{ beats per minute} \end{array}$$

This is the formula recommended by the University of Michigan Center for Fitness and Sports Research. Although opinions differ over what is the "ideal" exercise pulse-rate range and how it should be calculated, physical educators agree that sustained vigorous exercise, for at least twenty minutes a day, three days a week, is the key to increasing your energy and endurance.

The following general rules also apply:

- Have a thorough physical examination if it's been more than a year since you've had one. It's important to be sure that your heart, lungs, and blood pressure are in good shape before switching your lifestyle from sedentary to strenuous.
- Begin slowly and build up gradually, or you'll risk injury, sore muscles, and acute disillusionment. If you're taking up running, start off with a mile walk; work up to a brisk walk/jog and finally to a sustained, steady run. To start off running is akin to entering the family car in the Daytona 500.
- Pick the right shoes. An Oleg Cassini warm-up suit is a nice touch, but proper footwear is mandatory. Let the local sports shop assist you with the right choice for your activity.
- A warm-up period is essential to loosen up your muscles and joints before beginning. Most people find that at least five minutes of *slow* bending and stretching, especially of the back and leg muscles, is good preconditioning. Likewise, include at least five or more minutes of slow, "cooling down" relaxation exercises afterward, as your pulse rate returns to normal. An illustrated fitness manual can show you which exercises are best for your particular sport.

That's just the formal part of your exercise program. Viewing yourself from now on as an "active person," you'll see every added movement as a coin in your fitness account. Exert yourself. It may not be practical to run to and from work every morning, the way Senator William Proxmire does, but perhaps you could bicycle. Or at least park a few blocks from the office. And when you get there, take the stairs.

At home, does it make sense to pay someone else to mow the lawn and do the heavy housework while you pay for using the exercise machines at Vic Tanny's? Think it over. If the do-it-yourself route takes twenty minutes longer but gains you twenty minutes of exercise, it's not necessarily poor time management. You're accomplishing two things for the price of one.

Cue yourself. Dorothy Harris, professor of health and physical education at Pennsylvania State University, suggests placing stickers on the refrigerator, the mirror, and the dashboard of the car as reminders to do isometric and tightening exercises. "As you drive, let every red light be a reminder," she advises. "Or practice your bends and stretches while drying off or dressing after a shower or bath."

Television presents a perfect background for calisthenics, jump-rope, or running in place. The commercials help you mark time. Trapped in a long-winded phone conversation? If nothing else, you can accomplish the day's toe touches and knee bends.

Involve the people you care about, and exercise becomes quality time as well. I am thinking of the confidences my eleven-year-old daughter and I have shared on long winter hikes; the good conversations with my friend Ruth between racquetball sets. Most "Y"s and community recreation centers offer reduced rates for families or other pairs, and for groups of applicants. Investigate them.

ZZZZZzzzzzzzzz

You don't tend to appreciate it until you've lost it: That indispensable good night's sleep. Without it you become edgy and apathetic, unable to think coherently or perform simple tasks. Sleep restores energy. Without it, you're operating on empty.

Sleep requirements vary from one individual to the next, but anything within a range of five to nine hours is generally considered normal. Experiment and find your own quota. If you're dragging by midday and exhausted all evening, try getting to bed an hour earlier each evening for a week, and see if it makes a difference.

On the other hand, if you find that you feel just as peppy and alert after seven hours sleep as you do with eight, think of what you can get done in that extra hour per day!

Adjust the pattern of your sleep to your lifestyle. "As a student I routinely stayed up until 2 or 3 A.M. because that was the quietest time in the dorm for studying," relates Anella, an advertising copywriter. "Now that I'm commuting to work in the city, my motto is 'early to bed, early to rise.' I have to beat the crowd and beat the traffic."

About a dozen of the women I surveyed listed "sleep" among their five top priorities. "It may seem odd to rank sleep above child care and paid employment," one commented, "but I can't function in any of my roles without it."

Close to one-third of all Americans aged eighteen and over perceive themselves to have "trouble sleeping," according to the Committee of the Institute of Medicine of the National Academy of Sciences, although only 2 percent of the cases are severe enough to be characterized as "insomnia."[3] Most sleeping problems can be traced to emotional stress: An anxious review of the day's events; more agitated anticipation about what will come next. And with each minute that passes, the desperate feeling that the more sleep you lose, the harder it will be to cope tomorrow.

"Sleep is such an important area of our life and so much attention is focused on it that when we don't sleep, we want the problem 'taken care of,'" notes Dr. Sonja S. Pinsky, a Toledo, Ohio, psychiatrist. "But while sleeping medications may help the symptom, they don't get to the root of the problem. Medication does not restore normal sleep." She explains, "Generally this medication becomes less effective with time and larger doses and larger doses are needed for the same effect."[4]

Instead try some of the following home remedies: Comfortable bedclothes; a firm mattress; and a room that is cool and well-ventilated. You can also try opening your window to natural sounds like chirping crickets and the rustling of leaves.

The longer you stay in bed without falling asleep, the more disturbed you will become, Pinsky warns. It is better to stay in bed less and consoli-

[3]"Sleep: You Can Have Lots More of It," *Connections* (Toledo), April 14, 1980, p. 4.
[4]Ibid. p. 4.

date your sleeping time. Napping during the day is a deterrent to sleep.

Watch your diet. A cup of tea or hot chocolate in the evening relaxes some people, but the caffeine keeps others awake. Alcohol, too, may act either as a sedative or as a stimulant. Alcohol-induced sleep is often disturbed and fragmented, Pinsky states, and should be avoided.[5]

If you're tense about problems at home or at work, block them from your mind with an engrossing (but not suspenseful) novel. Concentrate on something neutral, like tomorrow's grocery list.

Vigorous exercise, while it seems to improve people's sleeping in general, can be overly stimulating if it is done right before bedtime.

Try this relaxation exercise: Breathe slowly and deeply, from the chest. Stretch out to your full length and then relax. Now contract and relax each of your muscles, starting with the toes and working up to your nose. You should fall asleep in the process.

[5]Ibid.

16

Child's Play

"It's not the quantity of time you spend; it's the quality."

That phrase has numerous applications to time management, but it is most often heard in reference to time spent with children. Ten minutes of attentive concern is worth more than hours of indifferent proximity. A five-second hug builds bonds that last a lifetime.

"Quality time" has become almost a slogan for working mothers, who ferret it out between loads of laundry and trips to the supermarket. A small minority one generation ago, working mothers now number over 14 million. According to the U.S. Bureau of Labor Statistics, more than 50 percent of all women with children under eighteen are currently employed—compared with 19 percent in 1960—as well as over 40 percent of the mothers of preschool children.

As our ranks have increased, our doubts and defensiveness have diminished. Most working mothers today, whether employed by choice or necessity, believe that they *can* manage a career without grossly neglecting their families. Many are even convinced that children benefit, and not just economically, by having a working mother.

"I was miserable when I was home full time," says Rita, a department store manager. "I spent years picking up toys and hanging up clothing, feeling grouchy and unappreciated. My job has caused my kids to accept more responsibility and become more independent. And since working makes me a happier person, we automatically have a better relationship!"

Rita has noticed that since she is with her children less often, she enjoys their company more. She feels more sensitive to their disappoint-

137

ments and triumphs. "I'm more conscious of the time we spend together," she believes, "knowing that the time is limited."

Mothers who have chosen to stay home full time are just as aware of this limitation, although their perspective may be different.

Liz, whose daughters are now seven and ten, feels "nothing I will ever do is as important as raising my children. I don't want to miss even a minute of it, or make any compromises."

While Liz isn't drawing a paycheck, she would hardly be called unemployed. She has been a school volunteer, skating instructor, a Scout leader, and a lunchroom assistant, choosing jobs that allow her some proximity to her girls instead of taking her away from them. "You spend about one-fifth of your life raising children," she argues, "and then they are off on their own. I'll only be about forty when my youngest goes off to college. That leaves twenty-five years to pursue a career!"

So time itself is relative. It doesn't matter how much you have but how much you *think* you have and how you choose to use it. Twenty hours a week or twenty hours a day, you want the time with your children to be particularly well spent and rewarding, for both of you.

QUALITY TIME—ANYTIME

Quality time isn't something you give your child, like a birthday present. It's something you exchange. It's a combination of talk, thought, and activity during which you both feel close and comfortable. It can't be forced, especially at times when either of you is cranky or preoccupied. Yet it can occur at any time you're together, as long as the channels of communication are open.

What you do together isn't all that important.

Elise, a studio actress, gave up custody of her son when she was divorced five years ago, and sees him only on holidays and weekends. "I used to knock myself out planning trips to shopping malls and amusement parks. I wanted each of his visits to be a memorable occasion. One day the ball game we'd planned to see was rained out and we spent a whole Saturday afternoon in my apartment, doing nothing. For once we didn't talk about the 'event' that was taking place; we talked about ourselves. It was a turning point in our relationship.

"I realize that I want my son to look forward to seeing *me,* not some ball game or circus. Now I include him in more of my day-to-day activities. I still take him to the movies, but also to the laundromat!"

Most parents agree that it is the ordinary activities and everyday give-and-take that mold a relationship. Think of ways to include your child in your world. As you cook, give your toddler a bowl and a wooden spoon to stir with. Let an older child help by scrambling the eggs or tossing the salad. Virge, thirty-four, a registered nurse, turns routine errands into "adventure and discovery trips" for her four children, pointing out interesting landmarks and sights as they drive across town.

Repairing a table leg, planting a garden, washing a car: Your most mundane chores can, when shared with a child, become a special experience. Never mind that it's faster and easier to work by yourself. By incorporating your child's companionship, you're accomplishing two things at once.

"Children need parents, not pals," most psychologists say. There is no pressure on you to double-date with your teenager, or to climb into the playpen and build block towers all afternoon with the baby. On the other hand, it doesn't hurt to occasionally bend down to their level to help cut out paper dolls or join in a game of Monopoly. Shared activity, whether it's work or play, generates conversation, and nothing is more basic to good communication than talking.

PUTTING IT INTO WORDS

How do you talk to your child? Can you confide in each other about feelings? Hopes? Disappointments? We want to have a good rapport with our children, yet how often the dialogue seems to degenerate into a string of nagging reminders on our part and excuses and denials on theirs. Take notes, or even a tape recording, some hour and find out how much of your talk consists of, "When will you learn to..."; "Why haven't you...?"; "How many times must I tell you to...?" Is this really how you intended to spend "quality time" with your children?

Dr. Haim Ginott opened new doors of communication in his best-selling book *Between Parent and Child.* He stressed the importance of mutual respect and of statements of understanding that *precede* statements of advice or instruction.

When a child is angry or upset, it is not helpful to try to reason with him, Ginott says. The child wants sympathy, not constructive criticism.[1] Billy, nine, flew into a rage when he saw that his three-year-old sister had broken his model airplane. His mother could have said, "Calm down, you know it was an accident. Don't act like such a baby; it's only a toy. You can build another one." Instead she took his side. "That's too bad," she said. "You must really be furious. I know how hard you worked on that." In the end, Billy was reassuring his mother that it wasn't one of his favorite models anyway.

Communication is a two-way street. One way to encourage your children to confide their feelings in you is to be direct and candid with them. Tell them if you're worried or angry or upset. Don't burden them with intimate details of problems they have no control over—it's enough to say, "I'm a little on edge because I've had a rough day." This at least reassures them that *they* are not the cause of your behavior, and prevents them from blaming themselves. It also gives them an opportunity to express support and sympathy for you—a satisfying experience even for a three-year-old. It is important for your children to understand that you, like they, have problems—and that you can handle them.

Clear, honest communication is intrinsic to both the ideals of quality time and to time management. A family, like any organization, relies on free expression and cooperation among its members in order to function smoothly. Parents and children need to know what each expects of the other. Children should be informed when they make a mistake and praised when they do things right. Hurt feelings and minor dissatisfactions should be aired immediately so that they do not fester and grow into a needless crisis. In an atmosphere of tension and discord, little gets accomplished.

RESOLVING CONFLICTS

Suppose that at this point your family communication channels are full of static. You and your son seem to be constantly at odds with each other over his undone chores and sloppiness. Your most reason-

---

[1]Dr. Haim G. Ginott, *Between Parent and Child* (New York: MacMillan Publishing Co., Inc., 1965), pp. 25-26.

able requests end in a shouting match. At the opposite extreme is your daughter, compliant but uncommunicative. She is either off doing things with her friends or holed up in her room with the door shut. In the rush of your separate worlds, you seem to have lost contact.

How do you deal with these situations?

1. *Confront them.* Don't put it off by deciding that your children are "going through a phase" or that "things could be worse." Don't waste time feeling guilty or wondering if *you* are doing something to cause their behavior. Find out.

2. *Pick the right time.* Don't attempt a serious talk when your kids are groggily sitting down to breakfast or about to tune in their favorite television show. Nor should you be tired or tense or preoccupied. The dinner hour is often conducive to a thoughtful discussion.

3. *Don't accuse.* Simply state the situation as it exists, explaining that it creates problems for *you* and that you need their help in finding a mutually acceptable solution.

   "George, it makes me angry that you must be constantly reminded to pick up your things when you're finished with them and to keep your room in order. It makes the house messy and unpleasant for the rest of us."

   "Nancy, I really miss you since you've begun spending so much time alone or with your friends. I understand that you need your privacy, but it is important to me that we spend time together as a family.

   "What do you think we can do about it?"

   These statements are clear, direct, and to the point. Instead of stressing blame ("Why are you so inconsiderate?") they present your feelings. Most important, they enlist the child's help in resolving the problem.

4. *Listen.* "I should be able to keep my own room any way I want," George may argue. "John's parents don't make him do anything around the house." And Nancy: "After being at school all day I have homework to finish and hardly any time as it is for a social life. You're always busy with something anyway. Besides, what is there for us to talk about?"

   Be attentive at this point, and put the lid on your own grievances. This is the time for airing, not arguing. Let the kids have the floor.

5. *Generate solutions.* For George, these might include: (1) Easing up on the daily room straightening in favor of a thorough cleaning on weekends; (2) Rotating jobs, so that trash emptying alternates with loading the dishwasher or helping prepare dinner; (3) Changing territory: Instead of performing indoor duties, George assumes full responsibility for mowing and raking the lawn; (4) Agreeing on incentives, penalties, or both; for example, no television until chores are finished.

To create more time together, you and Nancy might consider such alternatives as: (1) Rearranging your schedules so that you're home together more often on evenings and weekends; (2) Planning a special event once or twice a month for the two of you, such as lunch at a restaurant; (3) Learning something new that interests you both, such as horseback riding, pottery, backgammon and so forth; (4) Preserving a special time during the day, perhaps just before Nancy goes to bed, when you are accessible to each other to talk over events, feelings, and problems.

It is important to suggest a variety of possibilities—even unlikely ones—to demonstrate that every problem has a number of solutions. As many ideas as possible should come from the kids. To encourage their input, don't praise, belittle, or pass any kind of judgement on any of their ideas until all have been submitted.

6. *Evaluate the solutions.* You and the involved child now agree on one or more solutions that are acceptable to both of you. The solutions accepted needn't be permanent; give them a trial period of a few days or weeks, and make adjustments if necessary. Be sure to follow-up at some later date by evaluating the outcome together.

These steps follow the "no-lose method of conflict resolution" endorsed by clinical psychologist Dr. Thomas Gordon in his workshops on Parent Effectiveness Training.[2] They work because they stress problem analysis, negotiation, and a mutually agreed-upon settlement. There is no room for criticism, blame, ridicule, preaching, pleading, or power plays.

It comes as a revelation to many parents, Gordon says, that there is an alternative to the traditional way of resolving differences, in which one side has its way and the other gives in. Parents needn't choose between being authoritarian or permissive; children needn't become either subjugated or spoiled. In a negotiated settlement, with both sides showing care and respect, everyone wins. It works between General Motors and the UAW, and it works between parents and children.

A good rapport, established during the preschool and elementary years, will help sustain your relationship with your children through the rockier years of adolescence. That's when the child who always thought you were brilliant and faultless perceives that you're not—a positive step toward a more realistic, comfortable relationship. Bombarded by disconcerting physical changes, peer pressures, and encroaching independence,

[2]Thomas Gordon, *P.E.T.: Parent Effectiveness Training* (New York: Peter H. Wyden, Inc., 1970).

teenagers need an adult they can level with; one who will offer them a sense of stability and support.

But whatever the child's age, parents have to feel their way along in conveying a degree of attentiveness that makes a daughter or son feel secure but not suffocated. Children of all ages need freedom and privacy. The absentee mother, whether she's been gone on a week-long business trip or an afternoon bridge game, may be tempted to overcompensate by spending every minute of her time at home in the child's company. It's not necessary. Togetherness, like all good things, has a saturation point.

For four years since her divorce, Marlene, thirty-nine, has shared a small apartment with her eleven-year-old daughter, Devrie. They are very close, yet each is sensitive to the other's need for time spent alone. "When I pick Devrie up after school, there's an outpouring of news between us, nonstop. Once we get home, I may go off by myself to fix dinner, and she retreats to her room and shuts the door. We're not rejecting each other. I think we each need some time alone to unwind. Silence is restorative. We have some of our best conversations—not just about happenings but about *feelings*—after spending some time alone."

Communication is more than spoken words. It is any action that conveys mutual respect for one another's needs. As children learn to value time to themselves, they are more likely to understand when you explain that you're tired. You'd like to sit and read the newspaper. You'll be available to them when you're finished with what you're now doing.

BUILDING A RELATIONSHIP

Four hours a day. That's the maximum time that Claire, a bank officer, has with her four children. An hour per child. "And not all of that is 'quality time,'" she observes grimly. "The hour before school every morning is absolute chaos."

Widowed three years ago, Claire eyes her evening hours like a frugal investor a tight budget. Time spent with her family gives her the "highest return," so she rarely gives it up to attend a meeting or social function. She is relishing these peaceful years, the "eye of the storm" between the more hectic stages of nursery and high school. The children, aged seven to twelve are "helpful and cooperative. The oldest babysits for the younger three after school, and everyone pitches in around the house. They have more responsibilities than many of their friends," she observes, "but they also have more self-reliance."

Claire has created more time for her children, and for herself, by teaching them skills of self-maintenance. "Even the youngest can operate the washing machine, cook parts of a meal, and keep his own room straight," she boasts. "I don't enjoy being a disciplinarian. I prefer to stress self-discipline instead.

"Being both a mother and breadwinner requires some compromises," she concedes. "I turned down a promotion in the bank's main office because it would have meant longer working hours as well as a thirty-minute commute. My position at the branch office is close to the children's school in case of an emergency.

"Our watchword is 'simplify.' We buy carpets that don't show dirt, clothes that don't need ironing, and foods that are quickly prepared. If a dinner of frozen pizza gains us an hour to go sledding before bedtime, I call it a good investment!"

Claire's family-versus-work time pressures seem exorbitant because she has a large number of children and is a single parent. Yet other mothers have comparable constraints. They work the night shift, or go to college full-time, or run several businesses from their homes, or have two-year-old triplets. Each lifestyle has elements that seem to make quality time hard to come by. Don't dwell on such elements. Just look for ways to work around them.

Here are some strategies for building close, comfortable relationships with your children, even on days with only minutes to spare:

- Be demonstrative. Children get messages not only from words but from a touch, a squeeze of the hand, from eye contact. A message has more impact, psychologists say, when its conveyed through more than one of the senses. A hug is universal language for "you're special to me."
- Rituals are an important part of childhood. Besides lending some order and consistency to the daily routine, they assure the child that at least once during the day, such as at bath- or bedtime, he or she will have your undivided attention.
- Especially at bedtime, the child needs a few moments alone with a parent, to unload his or her thoughts and worries; to feel loved and secure. This is the time to resolve petty arguments, not to generate them with a shouting

match over fifteen extra minutes of television. And long after they're physically old enough to independently hoist themselves under the covers, children need to be tucked in. This simple act of affection makes bedtime something to be looked forward to, instead of delayed or dreaded.

- Put a limit on television. American children are said to spend more time in front of the TV than they do in the classroom. That leaves little time for creative thinking or communication. Short of pulling the plug altogether, you could be selective about the programs you permit your children to watch, and you could watch with them. Then the TV can stimulate conversation instead of suppressing it.
- Old photographs, slides, and movies can also elicit pleasant talks about shared experiences and other memories. Children love to hear stories about your own childhood ("Were there dinosaurs back then, Mom?"). Plan a family trip sometime that enables you to point out your old school or neighborhood, or perhaps relive some favorite vacation from your childhood.
- Share your present world with them also. Take them to your office, or campus, or to the place where you do volunteer work. If possible, introduce them to your co-workers and explain what you do. A young child feels more secure knowing where you are when you're not with him or her; an older child benefits from early exposure to the adult world.
- Let your children know that you find their world equally interesting and important. Never underestimate how much they count on your presence at the end-of-the-year school picnic, or how proud they are to see you skillfully slicing the watermelon. There are bound to be times, especially if you're employed, when you can't drive for the field trip or you're late for the Christmas concert. But these will be easily forgotten if your children know that on other occasions you've come through.

Finally, beware of guilt, an emotion that attacks both working and nonworking mothers with a vengeance. We idealize a mother in a pinafore apron, kneading bread dough with one hand and wiping her child's tears with the other. She is always cheerful, loving, thoughtful and, above all, *there* when she is needed. She is a figment of everyone's imagination.

By trying to live up to this image—and inevitably failing—we risk our own mental health and that of our children. Children do not want a parent who feels guilty and apologetic. They feel safest with a parent who is secure in her actions, and who is self-confident.

Worse yet, if you try to assuage your guilt by offering your children special gifts and favors, you'll convince them that you must indeed be cheating or mistreating them. They will begin to expect these compensations, and soon you'll feel more guilty and inept than ever because you're raising spoiled children.

17

The Search for Mary Poppins

Whether you're an employed mother recruiting a forty-hour-per-week nanny or a homemaker in search of an occasional sitter or preschool program, you can't underestimate the importance of securing the right caretaker for you child.

What is important, most pediatricians and psychologists agree, is that the child be with a warm, loving adult; not that the adult be the mother.

Allow yourself a period of weeks to interview sitters, visit day-care homes or centers, and check references. Seek recommendations from other parents. The time you invest before making a decision will pay off, in peace of mind, in the long run. Don't compromise. It is imperative that you and your child both be comfortable with the person(s) he or she will be spending time with. Unassured that your child is well cared for, you won't be able to do your best work. And your child could suffer in a merely custodial situation.

Most working mothers agree that the ideal child-care arrangement is with a close relative living next door, who shares precisely their values, temperament, and lifestyle. Since such individuals are as scarce as fairy godmothers, you will probably find yourself hiring a stranger for this important task.

Having a sitter who comes to your home is probably the most convenient child-care arrangement, especially if you have an infant. This alternative is expensive, but many parents feel that the peace of mind it gives is worth the price. It's a temporary investment, ending when the child reaches school age. However, don't count on finding a sitter who will also do the housework. Generally speaking, the type of person who enjoys keeping a house clean, who is meticulously neat and well-organized, is not the type who likes to romp on the floor with a baby.

Nursery schools and day-care centers can provide interesting new experiences and social contacts for the child of three years or older, but be aware that these facilities range from superb to dreadful. Never choose one without visiting it with your child and talking at length with the director, staff, and other parents. A less overwhelming environment, especially for the child under three, might be with a neighbor who cares for a few children in her home. This is less expensive than having a sitter come to your house, yet provides the child with a consistent substitute mother and regular playmates.

As a time consideration, try to choose a day-care setting that is near your home or work place. Your mornings will be rushed enough without the added pressure of a long commute. A place that is on the route between your home and office is ideal.

Whatever system you choose, make sure the child is part of the decision-making process. Observe how the child and the caregiver act toward each other, and respect the child's instincts as well as your own. It isn't difficult to sense whether a person wants this job strictly for the income or because he or she genuinely likes children.

Other things to keep in mind, whether you're considering a relative, a day-care center, or a day-care home are:

- Are the persons who will spend time with your child stimulating? Will they answer questions, read books, encourage curiosity? Are they flexible? A caregiver should be neither overly permissive nor very restrictive. Instead, the person should be sensitive to the child's individual needs and be able to negotiate.

- Will your child be isolated, or will he or she be exposed to a variety of people, possibly of different ages and backgrounds? Are there enough adults in proportion to children to permit the adults and children to get to know one another well?
- Does the environment offer a variety of play areas: Large open areas for running freely; a space for messy activities, such as fingerpainting and mud-pie making; quiet corners for privacy and rest?
- Are there toys for creative play, such as art supplies and dress-up clothes? What about motor activity? Are there tricycles, jump-ropes, a swing set? If you're bringing your child to a neighbor's or relative's home, you can offer to supply those toys that are lacking.
- Is it safe? Are medicines, cleaning supplies, and other harmful objects out of reach? Are there gates across stairways and covers on electrical outlets? Is the outdoor area fenced in or removed from traffic?

Securing good, reliable child care is the single greatest hurdle a mother must cross in deciding to return to work or school, or in pursuing some other interest. A day-care center can have credentials that rival Harvard's; a sitter can produce references from the President and his cabinet, and the conscientious parent will still reserve judgement until she's sure the child's needs are satisfied.

If children are not happy in a particular care situation, they'll let you know by their reluctance to go there. A change in behavior that includes combinations of depression, withdrawal, tantrums, clinging, increased bedwetting, or frequent nightmares should be taken as a warning that something is wrong. These symptoms must be dealt with, or all of your motivation and energy will be absorbed in worry and guilt. Working and mothering are demanding enough when everything is running smoothly.

The day to look forward to—though it may be a bit hard on your ego—is the one when your child is as happy to see his or her friends at the sitter's or day-care center as to see you and return home. This is equally true for the nonemployed mother who is apart from her child for shorter durations. A separation from you for a reasonable length of time can expand your children's world, not diminish it. They'll develop a sense of confidence in new situations, learn to get along with other children, and discover the reassuring truth that parents are not the only adults who like and care about them.

THE AFTERSCHOOL SHUFFLE

Once the children are settled in elementary school, your child-care problems are over, right? Right—from about 9 to 3:30. Unfortunately, you may be expected to be at work from 8 to 5. Some communities have developed innovative early-morning and afterschool programs, but the majority of schools remain out of sync with the schedules of working parents.

Infants and preschoolers can usually adapt to any warm, friendly care situation. But older children, not surprisingly, tend to be choosier about what they want to do and whom they want to do it with. And who can blame them? They spend most of their day at school following the teacher's directions. Now they want some time to themselves.

Our family has been grappling with this problem since our children began elementary school, and in seven years we have tried a slew of solutions. I share them here in no particular order of successfulness.

- Your child can go to the home of a friend after school and play there until you pick him or her up. But there are several drawbacks: (1) This is a big favor to ask of another parent, and you can hardly compensate by offering a babysitter's wages. I try to make a reciprocal arrangement, such as caring for the other mother's children in the evening or on weekends. (2) If you have more than one child, the odds are against finding another parent anxious to take on all of your brood. That could mean negotiating with several parents. (3) Even if the children do all get along together now, they probably won't two months from now. Familiarity breeds contempt—in all ages.
- The arrangement with your child's friend's mother is probably doomed for another reason. She's been looking for a job herself. You can bet that as soon as you and she have established a secure, steady arrangement, she will hit you with the happy announcement that she starts work on Monday.

  On the positive side, you and she might pool your finances and hire a babysitter for your combined offspring; however, this works only if you can find an extremely reliable teenager or college student whose classes happen to let out at the same time as the elementary school.
- Take advantage of programs offered by the "Y" or community recreation center. We have productively filled many 4- to-5 P.M. time slots with lessons in swimming, the trampoline, and arts and crafts. However, fees

mount rapidly for these eight-week activity sessions—and you still have to find a way to get the kids from school to the place where the lessons are held.

- Finally, your child could join you at your workplace during the last part of the day. This is feasible in some settings (for example, if you work in a public library) and impossible in others. In general, I find "going to Mom's office" is best reserved for special occasions, and not made a daily routine. Your children will have a much more positive image of your job if they're not overexposed to it. (The same goes for your boss and co-workers and their exposure to your children.)

CAN THEY STAY HOME ALONE?

With so many potential complications and drawbacks in almost any afterschool arrangement, it's no wonder many parents opt for letting the children take care of themselves. This practice is widespread among parents I've interviewed. Some children are left at home alone for short periods of time at as early an age as seven, and many are caring for younger siblings by the time they are eleven or twelve.

This arrangement saves considerable time and money. No more shuttling back and forth to activity centers and sitters. No more negotiating fees and reciprocal trade-offs. It may cost you some initial uneasiness, however.

All mothers and fathers leaving their children at home alone for the first time report the same experience: trepidation, followed by increasing pride and confidence as the children prove themselves self-reliant and responsible. This is not to say that the parents don't worry and take measures to ensure their children's safety. They set strict rules. Among the families I surveyed, the following instructions to children are typical:

- *Never tell a phone caller the parents aren't home.* Instead, the youngsters are instructed to say something like, "My mother can't come to the phone right now. May she call you back?" The child can then call the mother at work and give her the message.

  Some children are not permitted to answer the phone unless it's the parent's ring—a prearranged code such as one ring, followed by a pause, and then another ring. Parents always post a list, by the phone, of the numbers where they can be reached, the telephone numbers of neighbors who are usually home, and emergency numbers such as those of the police and fire departments.

- *Don't open the door to strangers.* A one-way safety mirror, through which the child can see who is knocking without opening the door, is a good security measure. Again, the child does not announce, "My parents aren't home," he or she just doesn't answer at all.
- *No friends in the house.* The rationale for this, most parents say, is that the more children you have on the premises, the higher the chances of trouble. "I trust my daughters and I trust their friends," says Barbara, an elementary school teacher. "But if I weren't home and there was an accident, I'd be responsible. I feel more at ease having just my own two to worry about."
- *First the chores, then the television.* Knowing well the association of idle hands and Satan's mischief, most of the parents I talked to outline specific tasks for their children to complete while home alone. Homework is the first order of the day. Emptying the dishwasher, setting the dinner table, and practicing music lessons are typical additions. Some children receive money for doing extra chores, or for supervising younger sisters and brothers.
- *The use of appliances is restricted.* Parents are justifiably cautious about permitting young children to use the stove, electric irons, or anything else that could cause a fire. But a ten-year-old can put a roast in the oven at an appointed hour, and many a thirteen-year-old takes total responsibility for preparing the family dinner. Laundry is another area older children manage easily. And what a time-saving boon to a working mother—to come home and find a hamperful of wash all clean, sorted, and folded, instead of facing it on the weekend.

How do you know if your child is mature enough to be left alone? There is no magic age of readiness, and each mother must make her own judgement. Often the child will bring up the subject, indicating that he or she has been giving it some thought and feels willing to give it a try. This is a good sign because you want your child, when left alone, to feel cautious but confident—not frightened. The proximity of neighbors is an asset. Although my friend Kathy, a single parent, must be at work thirty minutes before her seven-year-old son leaves for school, she is reassured by knowing that the couple in the other half of her duplex are home and within earshot in case of an emergency.

You can ease into the situation. Gary and Liz began leaving their two daughters, then aged nine and seven, alone in the early evening when they went jogging. It was still daylight, the neighbors on both sides were home, and the girls felt perfectly at ease playing inside by themselves. At first Gary and Liz just circled the block a few times. Then they began going longer distances as they saw that the girls were getting along fine by themselves. Eventually they had no qualms about leaving the children when they went out for an evening.

No, scratch that. Parents always have qualms. It goes with the territory. But we can go a long way toward alleviating our worries by keeping in close telephone touch with our children. And those phone calls, along with cheery notes or perhaps tape-recorded messages, let the kids know that whether we're in the next room or across town, we care just as much about them.

Undoubtedly there are children who dislike being left alone, but the ones I've talked to take pride in their independence. They don't feel neglected. In the best of these arrangements, the jobs that the children complete after school, such as setting the table and starting dinner, help create more time for the family to spend together after the parents arrive home.

Quite unanimously, children who are "pulling their weight" in the household feel capable, dependable, and very good about themselves.

18

Help From Your Children

When Helen had three babies in less than three years, her friends were dismayed. "Poor thing," they tittered, "they'll run you ragged." "Nonsense," she smiled confidently through a mouthful of diaper pins. "I'm raising my own live-in help!"

Hopeless idealism? Not at all. In homes across the country, children *do* automatically make their beds before coming to breakfast; do set the table without being asked four times; do volunteer to mow the grass; and never fail to replace the empty roll of toilet paper.

But these children keep a low profile. The more noticeable kids are those who will do anything to avoid helping around the house. Especially when those kids are our own.

Why are chores an accepted part of the routine in some families and a source of constant contention in others? The difference seems to lie more in parental expectations than in child capability.

Helen, for example, was raised in a large family where everyone pitched in. Many hands make light work. While there was plenty of work to be done, it was eased by a spirit of cooperation and fun. "More

155

than a burden, chores were something we felt entitled to," she recalls. "There was status associated with the ability to do certain tasks. It proved we were trustworthy and capable."

The parent who tries to "do everything" for her child may imply the opposite—that the child is incompetent. Or she may criticize or redo a child's job because it is not up to adult standards, thus discouraging the child's future efforts. The child who fails to win approval by being helpful may try other ways of getting attention—such as by being obstinate. Thus, whether from being too demanding or too lenient, the mother who engages in such practices is left to do everything herself.

THE MYTH OF THE GOOD MOTHER

The parent-as-servant is rather a recent phenomenon. In pioneer days, children worked shoulder-to-shoulder alongside adults. They helped clear the land, care for livestock, harvest the crops. As society became more urban and industrialized, children often took jobs in the factories or as skilled apprentices, besides pulling their weight at home.

But the postwar and prosperous fifties saw a new division of labor. Men became the sole breadwinners while their wives took over almost exclusively the cooking, cleaning, and other housework. Home appliances reduced much of the drudgery of these chores, and sociologists heralded the emergence of a new "leisure class." In many families, the "leisure class" was the children.

"We were a generation caught in the middle," says Sybil, a grandmother in her sixties. "As children we minded our parents, and as parents our lives revolved around our children.

"I would like to have found a job, but how could I, I rationalized, and still be home when the kids got home from school? Instead I plowed my energy into volunteer work and chauffering them to music lessons and baseball practice. The housework? They were too busy with their own friends and activities. I arranged my schedule to accommodate theirs and avoided making demands on them."

Many of us were raised by such women as Sybil and fell into the same pattern as she did. Some of us were so conditioned that even after taking full-time jobs we felt compelled to continue baking home-made cookies and keeping the house spotless. We were determined that our work (and our absence) would impose no hardship on our children.

The Good Mother seems a laudable role model, sacrificing and selfless. But sooner or later this role wears thin. Instead of feeling needed, we feel exploited. Supermom becomes supermartyr, a grouchy lady who's no fun to live with no matter how tidy she keeps the place.

The outcome appears ironic in retrospect—those worries of the fifties that working mothers would produce shiftless, delinquent children. Among families I know, the effect has been just the opposite. Feeling that their contributions are needed, most children will rise to the occasion. Given responsibilities, they will become responsible.

In sum, there is no excuse for doing all the housework yourself, and there is a strong case to be made for sharing it among all the family members. It fosters in even the youngest children a sense of participation and self-worth. It also teaches children practical skills, from wielding a dustpan to turning raw eggs into a palatable breakfast.

If maintaining an orderly home makes you feel useful and important, why not give your children the same satisfaction?

As Claire, a working mother of four, puts it, "We're all in this together. We all share the roof over our heads, food, clothing, and other comforts, so we should all contribute to their upkeep. Everyone chips in because everyone benefits."

THE COOPERATIVE SPIRIT

Some families resort to elaborate charts and point systems to make sure that all members pull their weight; others operate smoothly on a less formal basis. The Robinsons, for example, devised a schedule of all household chores to be done on a daily or weekly basis, and assigned point values to each chore. Cooking dinner rates seven points; dusting counts as one. Each of the five children and the parents are required to earn a minimum number of points per day and per week.

The Irvings opted for a less structured system, simply talking over among themselves what must be done regularly, and asking for volunteers. After some experimenting, John, aged ten, has assumed most of the weekly tasks, such as trash collecting, because he can do them all at once and be free for several days afterward. His brother Frank, eight, agreed to set the table each night, but after two weeks he traded this task for the messier job of clearing the dishes afterward. This leaves him free to play outside until dinner is on the table.

Work sharing evolves slowly, families I've interviewed agree. It takes time to develop a system that all members feel is equitable. But when necessary, a crash program can also be effective.

Linda, thirty-five, had always done all of the family housework. Tamara, nine, and Adam, seven, were responsible for keeping their rooms straight. Linda's husband pitched in occasionally if guests were expected, but mainly confined himself to the yardwork. When the two were divorced, Linda realized that she would need both a full-time job to make ends meet, and help with her full-time responsibilities at home. "I sure couldn't afford to hire anyone," she relates, "so I turned to my most under-utilized resource—the children.

"I began by apologizing to them, not for dumping more work on them now, but for not sharing it with them sooner," she says. "It was my mistake, I explained, for failing to offer them a larger share in running the household and the chance to learn from the experience.

"We began a practice of sitting down together every Saturday morning after breakfast and making a list of all the jobs that needed to be done around the house that weekend. We break them down into small units—not 'clean bathroom' but 'wash around sink' and 'clean toilet,'" explains Linda. "Each person, including me, volunteers for six to nine jobs. We go right to work. They can't go out to play, and I can't get involved in other activities, until we're finished.

"Oh, there were problems at first. My son would stomp around and complain and slam himself into his room. About thirty minutes later he'd quietly emerge and finish his chores before anyone.

"In the beginning you lose more time than you gain—prodding and supervising," she observes. "And it certainly takes more patience to show a young child how to load the dishwasher than to do it yourself. But over time, the investment will pay off and you'll have responsible, independent children."

"*But I forgot*" runs an all-too-familiar juvenile refrain. How do you cope with the child who doesn't do his or her fair share? Instead of resorting to bribery, pleading, or punishment, try the method called "*logical consequences.*"

Through logical consequences, the child is allowed to continue an unsatisfactory behavior until the situation becomes so intolerable that he or she independently decides to correct it. The responsibility stays with the child (where it belongs) instead of bouncing back to the parent. There's no power struggle, just a straightforward learning experience.

Susan, aged eight, begged for a kitten and promised to take care of it. But she frequently left for school without feeding it, and forgot to empty its litter box. For a time, her mother covered for her rather than let the kitten go hungry or put up with the box's odor. But finally her mother said, "We won't be able to keep the kitten if you keep neglecting her." Susan promised to do better, but soon returned to her old habits. The kitten was then sent to live with Susan's cousins for two weeks. When it returned, Susan was much more conscientious.

The three Davis children were supposed to put their toys away each evening, but they usually took so long at it that they were up way past their bedtime. A shouting match ensued, with the children triumphant: "We're doing what you told us to!"

The problem wasn't the job but the timing. The Davises set an 8:30 P.M. deadline. Anything not put away by that time now goes into a large cardboard box and remains there for a week. The kids treated this as a great joke at first, but soon missed their belongings. Now they've made a game of the "beat-the-clock" cleanup. They even use the kitchen timer to add more suspense.

What distinguishes "logical consequences" from punishment is that the child is presented a choice and freely agrees to accept the results of his or her actions. This is also what makes the tactic more effective.

MAKING THE TEAM

Whether you're trying to launch or improve a family mutual-aid pact, the following principles are important:

Start when your children are young. Even a two-year-old can hang up his or her clothes, put away toys, help set and clear the table, feed the pets, and rake the leaves. "Preschoolers love to 'help,'" one mother observes. "Seize on that interest and reinforce it, even if the kids at that age are more of a hindrance."

Give children of any age a task they can succeed at and praise their efforts. Then, as their capabilities expand...

Let them choose. In any organization, members tend to perform better at tasks they volunteer for than at those they are assigned arbitrarily. Your son may be another James Beard in the making, and your daughter may much rather push the lawn mower than the vacuum cleaner.

Rotate the rejects. It's unreasonable to saddle one person week after week with scrubbing the toilet. The jobs that nobody wants should be passed around among all family members.

Each person should clean up after him- or herself. The main irritation in housework is not the annual stripping and resurfacing of the linoleum or any other monumental task; it's the open jar of peanut butter and the gooey knife left on the counter, or the jacket and school books flung on the living-room couch. Have you been plodding along this path of destruction, setting things right again?

No more. From now on resolve as a group: Don't put it down, put it away. Make it clear that if the food isn't put away after the snack, there will be no more snacks; that if the dirty clothes aren't put in the hamper at night, they won't get washed. The "clean-as-you-go-along" rule may take awhile to sink in, especially if you've been doing all the cleaning while the kids have been doing all the going. But stay firm. Logic and justice are on your side.

To each, his or her own. Everyone in the family should also be responsible for his or her own belongings. You can evoke this rule in those instances in which your child complains that *he* didn't scatter the train set all over the playroom, but that his friend Billy (who has since gone home for dinner) did. "Why should *I* clean it up?" he demands self-righteously. "Because it's your train set," you cordially respond. In the final accounting, ownership implies responsibility.

Be clear in your expectations and instructions. "Go clean your room" is a bit vague for a five-year-old; better to say, "Straighten the book case and put all the toys on the floor back into the toy box so I can run the vacuum cleaner."

Be realistic when you distribute the work orders, matching the job to the child's abilities. In the ideal script, the parent makes a reasonable request; the child does an acceptable job; the parent feels helped and expresses praise and gratitude, and the child feels proud, important, and appreciated.

Lower your standards. Picture this scene: Mom asks Bobby, aged seven, to rake the leaves. He works like a beaver making a mound four feet high. But when he calls her to show it off, she says, "That won't do at all. Look at all the leaves that are left!" Bobby feels deceived: He did what he was told, and all he is getting is criticism! He won't be eager to help in the future.

With young children especially, it's important to consider effort over results. This doesn't mean that you must settle for a fourth-rate job, however. Point out mistakes in an instructive manner: "Jill, you did a fine job on the dishes except for these few forks. If you soak them for a few minutes and then use the scrubbing pad, the food will come out from between the tines."

Be aware that some children will do an inferior job on purpose. Or that they will dawdle, fight among themselves, or in other ways become such a nuisance that you'll get exasperated and do the work for them. Don't go along with this game, or you'll soon find yourself the only participant.

A better tactic is to do the job *with* your child the first time or two, until he or she gets the hang of it, and to then put the child firmly in charge. Let the child know it's his or her self-reliance that you value.

Foster self-reliance with positive feedback. To the greatest possible extent, emphasize praise over criticism, incentives rather than penalties. Acceptance and encouragement build a child's self esteem and belief in him- or herself. Without this confidence, the child may not even *try,* much less succeed. Of course you have to be honest; you can't praise bad behavior or a job sloppily done. You *can* express dissatisfaction in a friendly and respectful tone of voice, showing that it's the deed you're rejecting, not the child.

The most effective way to influence behavior (see Chapter 4) is through rewards, not punishment. If you want your children to finish a task by 3 o'clock, you'll get better results by offering to take them to the movie when they're finished than by threatening to deny the movie if they're not.

Use rewards very sparingly, however, when it comes to housework. The attitude you're trying to foster is willing contribution, not "What's in it for me?" "Our children must learn to give without the ulterior motive of getting," says counseling psychologist Dr. Don Dinkmeyer. "At family meetings parents and children can plan the division and sharing of necessary household tasks. Through this sharing process, children learn cooperation and responsibility. They learn to work together for the good of all and develop values essential for healthy social relationships."[1]

CASH FLOW

Should children be paid for their work? Dinkmeyer and others argue that since parents are not paid for the jobs they do around the house, children shouldn't be either. Maintaining a comfortable home should be a sufficient mutual reward.

Another view holds that since adults receive a salary for the work they perform outside the home, it is reasonable to pay children for housework. Some families make up a comprehensive list of jobs and values (ten cents per room vacuumed; twenty-five cents for emptying the trash) in the belief that it will encourage self-motivation and industriousness. "But it can backfire," warns Bonnie, the mother of three teenagers. "Our children now believe they should be paid for *anything* I ask them to do, and they do as little as possible!"

A third option is the weekly allowance. This, too, parallels the work world, in that the child fulfills a certain number of agreed-upon duties and receives a regular income. But should the allowance be docked if the chores aren't finished? The consensus among child-rearing experts seems to be no. An allowance, like a salary, should be a sum that the child can depend on and plan with. Its purpose is to teach the value and management of money. If it can be revoked any time the bed isn't made properly, it's no longer a learning tool but a means of reward and punishment.

The solution is to dissociate expected chores from expected cash. If children do not follow through on their responsibilities, it is more suitable to restrict television programs or play time than to withhold the allowance.

On the other hand, it seems reasonable to pay extra for work "above and beyond" routine duties, such as washing the storm windows, waxing the car, or babysitting for younger siblings. "I'd be paying an outsider to do these things," one mother explains, "why not let

---

[1]Don A. Dinkmeyer and Gary D. McKay, *Raising a Responsible Child* (New York: Simon and Schuster, 1973), p. 63.

my own kids earn the money?'' The experience can pay off in more ways than one. One enterprising youth painted his parents' home, took "before" and "after" pictures, and printed up advertising flyers. He distributed them, with price estimates, in mailboxes throughout several neighborhoods. His growing business is helping to pay his way through college.

19

Beyond "Help" From Your Husband

Greg, thirty-four, arrives home from work and sees the breakfast dishes still on the kitchen table.

He feels mildly annoyed as he looks at the plates crusted with dried egg and toast crumbs. He feels impatient as he looks for a clear spot beside the table to set down his briefcase. He feels sorry that he lives in such an untidy house, and then he feels magnanimous as he decides not to complain about it to his busy wife.

What he doesn't feel is any impulse to clean it up himself.

When Debra, thirty-two, arrives home fifteen minutes later from her teaching job at a community college, she puts down her books, hangs up her coat, and begins to clear the table like a programmed robot. "Why is it that only I have this compulsion?" she asks herself, more amazed than aggravated. "We can both look at the same mess and one of us thinks, 'Gee that's too bad,' while the other feels instant responsibility and guilt."

The episode is far from unusual. Are these differences between females and males learned? Are they genetic? Most important, are they reversible?

165

Two people are at fault here: The man who does not instinctively do his fair shair *and* the woman who does not expect him to. They needn't be married. Even couples who are living together often find it easier to split the rent than the housework. Early social conditioning led most of us to believe that the house is mainly the woman's domain, just as paid work is the province of the man.

TRADITION DIES HARD

The "good mother" we tracked in Chapter 18 not only coddled her children; she served as errand girl, social secretary, laundress, cook, and scullery maid to her husband. Nor did she mind, necessarily. It seemed like a fair trade-off. He produced income for both of them; she contributed a comfortable, supportive environment.

Raised in such an atmosphere, many of us, male and female, have fallen easily into the same pattern. We could hardly have expected to behave differently. Mothers of the fifties and sixties dutifully taught their daughters to mix meatloaf and to iron daddy's handkerchiefs; their sons (who grew up to be our husbands) were excused to play baseball. School systems reinforced the traditional sex roles by routing the boys through industrial arts classes and the girls through home economics.

When women moved into the predominantly "male sphere" of the work force, men did not reciprocally stampede to the kitchen. No surprises there. Paid work offers financial, social, and personal rewards to women. Housework provides few comparable compensations to men.

In fact, men still find household chores a little demeaning (for themselves, of course, not for their wives). In 1980, when *The Wall Street Journal* conducted a news roundup on changing family roles, its reporters "repeatedly encountered men who were afraid to let their housework activities be known" lest their peers would make fun of them.

"Guilt, in fact, is a powerful motivator," the article stated, adding that "Many men readily concede that they would be content to sit back and bask in the glories that have been traditionally been bestowed on the breadwinner, if it weren't that their wives were out there winning bread too."[1]

THE HAND THAT ROCKS THE CRADLE

Men seem to be less reticent today about participating in child care than they once were—fortunately for their wives, their children, and themselves. Fading are the stereotypes of the macho male; the aloof authoritarian figurehead who doles out an allowance and discipline; the corporate climber who misses the third-grade pageant because he chose to work late at the office. A small but stable men's liberation movement has drawn attention to the nurturing side of the male personality. This movement was given a boost by *Kramer vs. Kramer,* the 1980 Academy Award-winning film exploring a father's initiation into single parenthood. *Kramer vs. Kramer* both legitimized and romanticized the father-as-mother role.

Some employers are beginning to acknowledge men's family responsibilities by providing more flexible work hours, job-sharing opportunities, and even maternity leaves for men. And many men, with their wives contributing to the family income, feel less pressured about their own earnings and job advancement, and show a tendency to put higher emphasis on their relationships with their wives and children.

Everyone benefits from this. I think one of the most positive outcomes of women's entry into the work force has been the creation of more "equal time" in parenting; rather than twelve waking hours with mommy for every two with daddy, the child tends to spend a balanced ratio of time with both parents. In cases of divorce, joint custody seems to offer a solid hope of preserving these parent–child relationships and reducing the burden of single parenthood.

If a husband does not participate equally in child-care, it could be that he isn't given an equal opportunity. The same social conditioning that classifies males as "primary breadwinners" marks women as "pri-

[1]"Man of the House: More Working Wives Expose Their Hubbies to the Joys of Cooking," *The Wall Street Journal,* October 16, 1980, p. 1. Reprinted by permission of *The Wall Street Journal,* © Dow Jones & Company, Inc., 1980. All rights reserved.

mary parents." We are too quick to assume it's the mother who should stay home from work with a sick child, or supply cupcakes for the Little League picnic. We usurp responsibilities that should be shared equally.

I made this discovery several years ago, when a friend and I were planning to attend a meeting during which our husbands would babysit for us. "Wait a minute," said Candace, "do you hear yourself? When you stay home with your children do you call it 'babysitting'? Why are we saying our husbands will 'babysit' with their own children?!"

I realized then that I was giving my husband an "outsider" status—and rather unfairly, since he has always spent as much time with our children as I have. Even now I have an embarrassing tendency to presume that *I* will attend the parent–teacher conference or drive the carpool car, only to find out that he has been planning to do these things also. Why shouldn't he, he points out. They're his kids too.

SHARE AND SHARE ALIKE

There is a definite trend toward more sharing of domestic duties in this country. *The Wall Street Journal* said so; sociologists think so; my interviews with dozens of women bear it out. It's no revolution, they agree. Most often the new division of labor evolves slowly, after a child is born or after the wife returns to work or to school. Sometimes it takes a confrontation or marriage counseling. Ideally, simple logic convinces the couple that if both are contributing to the income, both should do the housework. Neither should feel overly put-upon, magnanimous, or grateful.

Young people in their twenties, or couples who married later after many years of independence, tend to be the most egalitarian. "He does the laundry for six months, then we switch," reports Gwen, twenty-six, a publicist who is married to a law student. "I'm responsible for cleaning above floor level; my husband mops and vacuums," says Kristin, twenty-nine. Many couples make meal preparation a togetherness time. One person does the main dish, the other puts together the vegetables and salad, and they catch up on the day's events as they work.

Couples in their mid-thirties or older often report a more traditional division of labor. "I do the laundry, shopping, cleaning, and cooking," explains Carole, thirty-nine. "Bill handles the finances, pays the bills, and does household repairs, maintenance, and yard work." Some women characterize this as a fifty-fifty split; others as a ratio of ninety-five-to-five. "Fair" is a highly subjective concept. Each couple must come up with a formula that both partners feel is equitable. "When we shared an apartment we cooked all our meals together and set aside an evening a week to do all the cleaning at once," says Jeanne, thirty-seven. "Since we bought a house, my husband has been putting in evenings and weekends on plumbing and rewiring, so I've assumed most of the meal-making and housework."

"Patterns of work-sharing *evolve* within a marriage," agrees Anne Marie, thirty-nine. "Your priorities and capabilities are much different in your twenties than in your forties. One of you may change jobs, or one of your children may pass through a phase which demands a greater degree of attention. You have to remain flexible. I am very skeptical of the concept of marriage contracts which set forth precise sets of rules and expect people to just plug into them."

During their fifteen-year marriage, Anne Marie and John have proven that there are numerous ways to balance family and career. John, a psychology professor, took full charge of the house and three preschool children for one year while on sabbatical to write a book, and Anne Marie worked as a research associate in a microbiology lab. At the midpoint of the year, they adopted a two-year-old Vietnamese girl; "proof," in their view, "that social agencies were becoming more open-minded toward nontraditional family arrangements."

During another recent year, when she was unemployed, Anne Marie painted and rehabilitated the upstairs bedrooms, refinished a piano, and volunteered as a Brownie leader, classroom tutor, and schoolroom parent.

Two years ago, Anne Marie traded the placid laboratory environment for a demanding and unpredictable job in real estate. It has meant new kinds of accommodations and helping arrangements among all members of the family. But as the work is shared, so is appreciation. "We tend to do what needs to be done without making a big deal of it," they explain, a philosophy that seems to run through many satisfying marriages. "John likes to cook and he's often home first in the evening, so it makes sense for him to handle most of the meals and grocery shopping. I supervise the laundry, which goes along with mending and buying clothes for all five of us. Mail order shopping is a great timesaver there," she adds.

Now aged eleven, twelve, and fourteen, the children do most of their own laundering and room upkeep, as well as yard work and other chores. "Child care" at this stage means a lot of nightly chauffering to music lessons and baseball practice. The available parent takes the wheel. "It's less a matter of whose turn it is than who will be least inconvenienced," John says. "Over time, I think our contributions come out to be pretty equal."

TOWARDS A NEW LABOR SETTLEMENT

If things don't seem exactly balanced on your end of the seesaw, don't just sit up in the air fuming about it. Resentment is debilitating, and right now you need your energy for more important things. Climb down and pipe up. Nothing is going to change as long as you suffer in silence.

Instead of seeing housework and child care as sources of contention, think of them as mutual commitments through which you may strengthen your relationship.

Letty Cottin Pogrebin, who has written extensively on changing sex roles, puts it this way:

> Housework is not trivial on any level. It even has an impact on future generations, for how housework is divided tells children how valuable males and females are and what their time is worth. Whether written or spoken, these tenets must be basic to every agreement:

1. Because a person earns more his (or her) time is not worth more.
2. The woman who earns less cannot be penalized twice: Once on the job (because of sex discrimination in wages) and again at home (where she is expected to do more housework).
3. No task is "inappropriate" or "humiliating"—there are only those which one is capable of performing, parent or child, and those one is not equipped to handle.[2]

[2]Letty Cottin Pogrebin, "There's More Than One Way to Slice the Pie...and Clean Up Afterward," *Ms.,* October 1979, p. 52.

You might begin by sitting down with your husband and listing the things that each of you does on a day-to-day, monthly, or seasonal basis. You will probably find that your list is not only longer than his, but that it is crammed with the repetitive daily and weekly chores such as cooking and laundry, while his contains more of those seasonal duties such as filing the income tax and tuning-up the station wagon. But while these jobs are important, they are also somewhat flexible—unlike making dinner. Try to trade a handful of your little marbles for a couple of his big shooters. Keep these points in mind also:

- In reallocating tasks, don't be hamstrung by the traditional stereotypes of women's work/men's work. Do what each of you finds tolerable and convenient. Rotate the jobs you both hate.
- Look after each of your own belongings, responsibilities, and appointments. Be practical, of course. There's no point in making separate trips to the dry cleaners for his topcoat and your wool skirt. But why should you schedule his dental checkup?
- While it is useful to keep switching around and experimenting, your main objective is to develop a routine. Routines cut down on an enormous amount of time spent relearning and remembering. To manage your time effectively, it is useful to know that all month long it's your husband's turn to drive to the nursery school, while Friday is always your night to make dinner.
- If your husband fails to carry out his end of the bargain, avoid the impulse to cover for him. This won't be easy, especially if you have a lower tolerance than he for a sinkful of unwashed dishes. Stay out of the kitchen, or better, stay out of the house.
- At the same time, be willing to compromise. You *could* say, "I see that you haven't gotten to the dishes. If you'll buy the groceries tonight I'll take care of them while you're gone."
- If you appreciate his help, say so. I agree with the feminist view that it's silly to fall all over yourself praising a man for doing the same chores women have done routinely for decades. But it still seems appropriate to thank someone for performing a service that benefits you. If you think about it, he probably shows his appreciation of you in other ways—by boasting about your recent promotion or surprising you with theater tickets for the weekend.

"If a man doesn't get positive feedback from his wife when he cleans the house or stays home with a sick child, he's not going to get it from anyone else," points out Bob, thirty-four, a Baltimore physiologist. Like his working wife, Bob is trying to strike a balance between his commitments to his two-year-old son and a demanding career. "But I can't really talk to anyone about it," he remarks. "My boss may respect me for wanting to spend time with my family, but he's not apt to promote me for it. He's more interested in an employee who works late in the lab every evening and weekend."

GAMES HUSBANDS PLAY...AND HOW TO OUTSCORE

You probably noticed that many of the foregoing points are similar to those outlined in Chapter 18. But dealing with your husband is not identical to dealing with your children. Little children tend to look to you for direction and are anxious to please. Besides, you're bigger than they are. Your husband or housemate may not welcome your new assertiveness. After all, the old you, subservient and compliant, was pretty easy to live with.

His resistance may take a number of forms. Some common ones may include:

"As long as I'm earning the highest income..." The man who equates money with power is likely to argue that because he contributes the most financially, his wife should contribute more manual labor at home. Couples who buy this theory should review their value systems. Again, why should a woman be penalized twice—through wage discrimination at work *and* more housework at home?

"I don't know how...." Many men enter a relationship with barely a passing acquaintance with any home appliance, other than the toaster. So you may feel like his mother in the course of pointing out manufacturer's laundering labels and the differences between various grades of beef. View the training process as an investment in your freedom. If little girls can be taught to unravel these mysteries, so can big men.

"All you have to do is ask...." This guy is just, well, unperceptive. You have just tripped over his outstretched feet, spilling an armload of the baby's toys, and as you bend over to pick them up he says, "Mind moving your head, honey? You're blocking the TV!" This man

will never figure out on his own that you need help. He has to be asked. Then he will say, "Why didn't you ask me sooner?"—leaving you to somehow feel foolish and incompetent.

"If your job is too much for you, you can always quit...." This is the most devious tactic of all: The suggestion that it's your problem, not his. His solution is for you to do less, not for him to do more. In this situation, be prepared to coolly state the reasons you *want* to be employed (unless you don't). They probably have to do with financial security, self-esteem, personal growth, new social contacts, and a more interesting life generally. Then counter with the suggestion that perhaps *he* should cut back on or quit *his* job in order to devote full time to keeping house.

Couples who reach an impasse over the housework should either pool their money and hire outside help, or resolve to live in a messy environment. Nagging, blaming, and harboring resentments are destructive both to you and to your relationship.

RELEASING CONTROL

If there is one advantage to being chief of domestic affairs it is that you can set your own standards. You get to decide what to do, when, and how to go about it. For all our rhetoric about equal sharing of household responsibilities, some women are curiously ambivalent about sharing control of them. The house is our turf. So instead of being delighted when our mate loads the dishwasher, we're apt to blurt out, "It's better to stack the cups along the side and the plates in the rear."

You don't need a Ph.D. in psychology to discern that if it's cooperation you want, criticism won't get it.

Ellen Goodman, syndicated columnist for the Boston Globe, wrote a thought-provoking column about household role-sharing. It described "The Grateful Wife" who for the first ten years of her marriage felt "lucky to be married to a man who let her work" (people talked like that in the sixties), and thankful that he was always willing to help with the house and the children. Goodman writes:

It's hard to know when gratitude first began to grate on my friend.... She began to realize all the items of their shared life were stored in her exclusive computer. Her queue was so full of minutia that she had no room for anything else.

"The Grateful Wife" began to wonder why she should say thank you when a father took care of his children and why she should say please when a husband took care of his house....

Her husband was not an oppressive or even thoughtless man. He was helpful. But helpful doesn't have to remember vacuum cleaner bags. And helpful doesn't have to keep track of early dismissal days.... Helpful is reminded. Helpful is asked.

The wife would like to take just half the details that clog her mind like grit in a pore and hand them over to another manager. The wife would like someone else to be grateful when she volunteered to take *his* turn at the market or *his* week at the laundry. The truth is...she doesn't want a helpful husband. She wants one who will share. For that she would be truly grateful.[3]

The column brought on a barrage of mail from Helpful Husbands. Most of them wanted to award the Grateful Wife an *Un* before her name, Goodman reported. In fact, "this modest proposal, that husbands take over management and responsibility of some of the workaday chores of their mutual children and homelife, elicited more response than anything I have written on the state of the world, immorality or immortality," she stated.[4]

The letters raised various arguments, including "Someone has to be in charge," and "Husbands have separate but equal duties such as weather-stripping and car care." But the most intriguing responses came from both husbands and wives, and had to do with "the much subtler problems of shifting responsibilities," Goodman wrote. "They had to do with power—the taking of and letting go of."

The letters included one from a Minnesota wife who worked out a system for sharing with her husband and then was dismayed to find him

[3]December 11, 1979, © 1979, The *Boston Globe* Newspaper Company/*Washington Post* Writers Group. Reprinted with permission.

[4]January 18, 1980, © 1980, The *Boston Globe* Newspaper Company/*Washington Post* Writers Group. Reprinted with permission.

"doing it all WRONG, which is to say he wasn't doing it MY way." When she confronted him with a long list of misdemeanors, such as not doing the dishes until after he'd relaxed with coffee:

> He told me that if he was going to cook and clean, he was going to do it his way and I had better butt out. I never realized how much I had invested in controlling these things and how much power I had over the real basics of life. It has taken ME a long time to learn how to share.

A man from Atlanta wrote:

> When my son was born I had every intention of taking half-care of him. But when I would change his diapers, my wife would come back and redo the pins. When I would feed him at night, she would go into the room after I was through and check on him. When I dressed him, she would say that his clothes didn't match.
>
> I decided that I had only two options: to get into a continual power struggle over the children or to let her take charge. I am now a "Helpful Husband." The irony is that I am writing to you because my wife put your article on my plate at breakfast this morning.[5]

For years, women's primary power was in the home, and we learned to exploit that power, to guard it fiercely. Now we find ourselves being drawn into new arenas of power where we feel less sure of ourselves. By holding tight to our old sources of domestic power, we retain a sense of control.

You have to lose to gain. Sharing entails not only taking on new roles but relinquishing old ones. It can mean feelings of insecurity for a time, but it can also lead finally to a sense of *real* control over *all* the important aspects of our lives.

---

[5]Ibid.

(20)
What Are Friends For?

It is 7 A.M. and Sandra, twenty-nine, has been up for an hour reviewing for the state bar exam, her ticket to a promising law career. She has been studying for weeks and feels ready and confident. Success seems right around the corner.

"Mommy . . . "

Four-year-old Benjamin is also right around the corner, and he is just waking up with "a terrible tummy ache." No way can he go to nursery school, he moans emphatically. "Why today?" Sandra thinks desperately. The law boards are only administered twice a year. If she misses today's exam, it will be six months before she can take it again.

By 8:30 Sandra has determined that her son is not sick enough for her to call the doctor, but not well enough to send to school. "It seems to be just a mild upset stomach," she explains to Michelle, a neighbor two houses away. "I'll be right over," her friend says without hesitation. "I was just planning a dull morning of hemming draperies." "I'm glad you said so," Sandra rejoined. "You can use my sewing machine."

Most often it's not a career or a child's health that hangs in the balance. It may just be a ride to work because your car is stalled, or a half quart of milk to save you a trip to the supermarket. Or it may be something intangible, like a reassuring phone call late some night when you're feeling despondent.

177

Physical or emotional, the support of a caring friend is not something women regard lightly.

"People ask me how I manage it all—a job, graduate school, and two kids," says Mickey, a thirty-four-year-old clerical worker, recently divorced. "I tell them I *don't* manage it all. I have friends, and we all help each other.

"There is a group of us in this apartment complex who have banded together," she explains. "We're all single, just getting established professionally, with harried schedules and practically no money. So we've pooled our resources. We exchange toys and clothing, share various appliances, watch one another's children. We are almost like an extended family.

"It gives me a great sense of security knowing I have people I can depend on," Mickey says. "But what's really rewarding is knowing that I am needed in return."

Such sharing comes naturally to most women, I think. We were brought up to be considerate and cooperative. Some of us have even made a career of being helpful, in such fields as teaching, nursing, or social work. Giving help is easy. The hard part is asking for it.

For some of us, calling for help seems to be an admission of failure. It's telling the world that we misestimated our capabilities and took on more than we could handle. We aren't Superwomen after all (and we really wanted to be). Humbled, we are now reluctant to ask for help for another reason: If we can't manage our own responsibilities, how will we ever be able to reciprocate?

These thoughts are irrational. The busier we get in this increasingly high-pressured, impersonal society, the more necessary it is to stop periodically and reevaluate what we're doing and how we're going about it.

Alone in a boat with one oar, you might be paddling in circles. With another rower, you can both make some distance. Bring a few more energetic people on board, and who knows how far you can go!

TAPPING YOUR SUPPORT SYSTEMS

"Networking" has become a catchword for those associations of career-minded women aimed specifically at furthering career goals. But in a broader context, networking applies to all those alliances we form to expedite our daily affairs. Sociologists call them "viable support groups." You probably call them family, neighbors, and friends.

What follows is an overview of some of the kinds of cooperative and sharing arrangements that go on in my hometown of Ann Arbor, Michigan. It's no national sample, but it is probably representative of the groups that function in your community. Look around and see what kinds of networks you can plug into—or organize your own!

Babysitting co-ops. Several babysitting pools operate in different geographic locations of the city. One of the largest involves some fifty families who exchange "points" for hours of child-care services. The arrangements are handled through a secretary (a position which rotates among the members) who fills requests for "sits" and keeps the record of how many points are paid and earned. Members with the most negative points are offered the sitting opportunities first, so that all members' point balances are kept near zero.

A smaller neighborhood babysitting co-op has about twenty members. This group arranges its own sits by calling people from a membership roster. Upon joining, a family receives twenty cardboard "tickets" which they exchange, rather than using a point system. And throughout the city, many neighbors babysit for one another's children on an informal basis, without keeping track of who owes whom.

As an alternative to teenagers, babysitting cooperatives not only save you money, but provide enormous peace of mind. Instead of spending hours trying to get hold of Jennie-down-the-street, who, it turns out, can't make it but can recommend her cousin's best friend who "really loves children," you trade time with another adult. You're assured of her experience and competence (she's a parent too), and you know that she won't cancel out at the last minute for a date with her boyfriend.

True, it costs you time when you babysit in return, but this time can be turned to your advantage. I find that the evenings I babysit for other families (once the kids are asleep), to be very conducive to catching up on reading or paperwork. In someone else's house, you're under no compulsion to jump up and do the dishes or water the droopy philodendron. You can treat your sitting time as "block time" to concentrate all of your attention on one project.

Playgroups. Even a toddler needs contact with people he or she can relate to as equals; people that can be seen eye-to-eye instead of eye-to-kneecap. And however enthusiastically you may have committed yourself to staying home with your child during the fleeting preschool years, you also need time to yourself. So scout around your neighborhood, church, or alumni group for women with children of similar ages who might be interested in forming a playgroup. Perhaps each of you could take turns caring for both of your children on a regular basis while the other has a few hours off to go speedily about her business, free of stroller and diaper bags, or simply to pursue work at home in peace and quiet.

In one such arrangement, four children, aged eighteen to thirty months, play together each Tuesday and Thursday morning, with the drop-off house being rotated every two weeks. "The day that it's my turn with four toddlers is pretty chaotic," admits one of the participants, "but I rather look forward to it. You get a whole new perspective of your child from watching her interact with others her own size."

As your children get older, these pooling arrangements become advantageous even for the parent in charge. One four-year-old will pester you to "Play with me, Mommy!" Two four-year-olds will play happily with each other. Two mothers in a New York suburb made this arrangement: Once a week, each picks up the children of both families from nursery school, feeds them lunch, and lets them play together until nap-time. The children enjoy the expanded time with a playmate, and each of the women gets a full seven hours a week free to herself.

Family mergers. If you're fortunate enough to know adults who your kids get along with, who perhaps have compatible children of their own, and who are sure to let you reciprocate, you can consolidate child-care for several days at a stretch. "My ten-year-old daughter thinks it's a great adventure to spend the weekend with her cousins when I want to attend a business conference," says Eileen, a single parent. "Instead of feeling left behind, as she would with a hired housekeeper, she gets to go someplace special too. And," she adds, "don't automatically rule out a close friend who has no children. Some of my unmarried friends have told me they welcome the chance to play surrogate parent."

Sharon and Pierre left their *four* children (all under the age of ten) with a couple of good friends who have four children of their own, and spent a week in Bermuda. "I don't need to tell you it was a great change of pace from our usual vacations in a camper rigged with six hammocks!" Sharon relates.

"We could never have afforded the round trip air fare for four children, and even a live-in babysitter for seven days would be an enormous expense," Sharon explains. "Besides, we feel it is a good experience for the children to become part of another household." Not intimidated at all by the prospect of caring for the crew in return, Sharon observes that "eight children can find plenty of ways to keep themselves occupied."

From my experience, it's easy to mesh extra children into your lifestyle for a few days if you stay loose, keep your sense of humor, and view the get-together as a kind of a house-party. The departing parents must supply written permission for medical treatment in case of an emergency; a key to their house; and, of course, a phone number where they can be reached at any time. The kids should bring a few favorite toys, along with clothes and sleeping bags. The hostess stocks up on popcorn and frozen pizza.

Carpools. "I thought life was hectic when I had to drive my children to and from the babysitter and nursery school," exclaims Joan, an Illinois mother of three. "I failed to anticipate the elementary/junior high period of music and dancing lessons; arts and crafts classes at the 'Y'; Scout meetings; catechism; ice skating and swimming lessons, and soccer practice. I feel like I'm spending half the day shifting between first and second gear!"

Unless chauffeuring bodies answers some deep-seated need for fulfillment, you and the rest of the parents on any carpool shuttle run should get together and consolidate your efforts.

Ask your child's activity leader (coach, instructor, or someone else) for a list of the class or team roster, and contact those parents who live around your neighborhood. "Carpools work only if all members are completely reliable," reminds one woman who has been organizing them for years. "It's no good if one person tends to 'forget' or is persistently late. Make sure there is a back-up plan if someone can't make it."

"The best thing I ever did was to open a charge account with a taxi service," suggests Anneke, a university development officer. "If I was caught in a meeting or for any other reason couldn't pick up a group of children who were expecting me, I could send a cab out to meet them. I didn't use it often, but when I had to, it was a lifesaver."

Grocery shopping co-ops. While not practical for filling the family's entire weekly food bill, a supermarket pool can eliminate some of those irksome midweek trips for just one or two items. Here are two possibilities.

> *Plan A:* Up to seven people living near one another each agree on a certain day of the week to do their grocery shopping. When a member of the group runs out of a certain item, she can phone the appropriate "buyer of the day" to add it to her market list.
>
> *Plan B:* Since weekends seemed to be the time that each ran low on certain foods (and were also the most inconvenient time to go shopping), four neighbors now take turns, each on one Friday per month, buying up to a dozen items for all of them. The participants phone in orders on Thursday evening and drop by on Friday night to pick up and pay for the items.

Cooking for a crowd. Instead of multiplying the recipe and freezing those extra lasagna casseroles, consider swapping them for main dishes prepared by your friends. "In our neighborhood, there are five of us who have each agreed to make enough food for all five families on separate weeknights. Around 6 o'clock, we bring our containers over to the cook-of-the-day's house and pick up tonight's meal," explains Kathy, twenty-eight, who organized the group nearly a year ago. She credits the project with "introducing lots of new foods to the family, especially international dishes. We're much more adventurous now in our cooking *and* eating."

Cooking once a week instead of nightly saves a lot of time, Kathy adds. Her husband picks up the night's meal on his way home from work. ("It's like having a private catering service," she says.) Since Kathy herself often doesn't get home from work until 6, she prepares the Monday evening meal on the weekend.

Another cooking co-op operates on a similar basis, except that it involves main dishes only, and all are prepared on the weekend. The members distribute the food on Sundays, and it is refrigerated or frozen until needed.

Swapping services. If you can outbake James Beard but can't thread a needle, and your friend hates to cook but can turn out a designer original on her portable Singer, why not trade your time and talents? "My neighbor and I had a great relationship," says Lila, fifty, a mother of five. "She did all my mending and alterations, and I sent over a freshly made pie or a loaf of bread whenever I did some baking.

It worked out beautifully because we both felt we were getting the best end of the deal!''

YOU'RE NOT ALONE

Stop and think for a moment about all your responsibilities. Are there areas in which you feel overextended? Problems that could be alleviated if only you had some help from another willing adult? Take the situation that puts you in the biggest time bind and see what you can do to improve it.

For me, it was the ninety-minute gap between the time that school lets out at the end of the workday. At ages six and nine, my children were too young to be home alone, and there were no available teenagers near our house who could babysit. I arranged a trade-off with a nonemployed mother so that on certain days my children would go to her house after school and on other days I would leave my office temporarily to drive hers and mine to the library or swimming lessons. Each of us benefits. She doesn't mind having extra children on several afternoons in exchange for not having to drive on the others. I am relieved to know that for part of the week I can work straight through the afternoon and know that my children are busy and cared for.

When you feel pressured and overwhelmed, don't hesitate to ask for help. Helpfulness is contagious. Once you approach people, you'll find there are plenty of others out there struggling with the same complicated life situations that you've got. They'll be happy to lend you a hand—and grateful to give you a chance to reciprocate.

21

You and You Alone

"On an emotional level, being single isn't always so great. But physically, when it comes to getting the things done that *you* feel are important, without interference—it's much more efficient," says Chris, thirty-one, a journalist and graduate student.

"After two marriages, I've decided it's easier to depend on myself," says Nancy, forty-two, a social worker with seven children.

"The disadvantages of being single, the aloneness, can also be to your advantage," observes Linda, thirty-eight, a medical writer with two children. "You don't have to confer with someone else about taking a job in another city, or even about the more routine things such as when to have dinner."

More and more women today, by choice or by chance, are confronting life alone. The statistics are self-explanatory. Women are marrying later. More than a third of all marriages end in divorce. Women outlive men by an average of eight years, and because of their greater age and number, widows are less apt to remarry than widowers. And many women, after establishing an independent and rewarding life and a well-paying career, are choosing not to marry at all.

Whatever their reasons, most of the single women I know view their status in a positive light. (Unlike some of my college dormmates, who saw singlehood as a holding pattern for marriage.)

185

In terms of time management, "aloneness" is a source of opportunity for personal growth and achievement.

Wholly on your own, you may sometimes feel overwhelmed by all of your responsibilities. But the burdens are offset by freedoms:

- Freedom from restrictive routines, such as someone else's work schedule, meal preferences, and so forth.
- Freedom to be yourself and play the life roles you are comfortable with, unrestricted by someone else's expectations.
- A social life you determine, doing the things you most enjoy with the people you want to be with.
- Financial independence. Your income may be smaller than that of most couples, but *you* determine how to spend it.
- Flexibility to travel, study, explore new ideas, and develop new areas of competence that increase your self-confidence.
- Opportunities to be jubilantly, peacefully *alone*.

NO PAIN, NO GAIN

Nobody will tell, you it's easy. Time management—indeed, life management—is a much different proposition for the woman who is single, widowed, or divorced. While married couples are grappling with the logistics of whose turn it is to cook dinner, she suffers no such conflicts. She has to do everything herself.

"Society puts single women at a double disadvantage," observes Marion, a widow with four children. "First, adult society is oriented to couples, so much so that the woman alone may be made to feel she is odd-one-out; one-half a unit rather than a whole individual.

"Second, society has fostered male and female role stereotypes to such an extent that many women are encouraged to develop 'feminine' personality traits and skills to the exclusion of masculine ones," she says. "So without a man around to perform certain tasks, such a woman feels inadequate and helpless. At greatest risk is the woman who is unexpectedly widowed or divorced, who had been brought up to believe 'I deserve to be taken care of. It's not fair that I should have to do everything alone.'"

Marion is one of the organizers of *Survival: For a Woman on Her Own*, a comprehensive workshop series assembled by the Michigan

State University Cooperative Extension Service. The course stresses the rewards and responsibilities of being on your own, especially the responsibilities to yourself. It urges that you:

- Take stock of your resources, including time, energy, abilities, attitudes, and money.
- Realistically assess the demands on these resources, such as your children, job, personal needs, and household-management requirements.
- View all situations in a positive manner. Think of change as a change for the better; a problem as a learning experience.

"Significant growth for human beings usually does not take place without a crisis," the workshop authors state. "Divorce, widowhood and living on your own for any reason can be the chance of a lifetime to adapt and develop new strengths, new attitudes and new freedoms as a result of weathering a storm."

Self-confidence evolves automatically as we acquire skills in unexpected areas and achieve success. It often follows hard on the heels of the realization that we don't *need* another person or specific material objects in order to find happiness and contentment.

Jeanne, thirty-seven, was in the midst of helping her husband, an able craftsman, restore an older home when the two decided to separate. "We both loved the house as a symbol of stability and of our marriage. I desperately wanted to remain a homeowner—in that house—because the image of myself as a rootless single renter was frightening. Yet I knew nothing about basic construction work," she says.

"I finally realized that I could keep the house, if I chose, by taking courses in remodeling or hiring someone to do the work. And that revelation—that I could choose to keep the house—freed me from the *need* to keep it. The house meant less to me than sharing the experience of working on it with my husband.'

"I'm a happy renter now, with an apartment big enough for me, yet small enough to keep under control."

For many of us, control over our living space is a fundamental aspect of control over our lives. As little girls, many of us were brought up to believe that home maintenance is a man's role, while our job is to keep the place tidy. That's not enough if you're living alone.

- If you don't know a hand drill from a crescent wrench, check out the courses available at your local community college or adult education unit and learn the basics of home maintenance.
- Invest in an illustrated step-by-step repair guide, such as Prentice-Hall's *Home Repairs Every Woman Can Do*. Such books cover everything from fixing a leaky faucet to pouring concrete. Just having one around may increase your feelings of security and competence.
- When you do decide to call a repair person, you should certainly shop around and get written estimates from several contractors before initiating the work. Seek recommendations from friends who have had similar work done in the past.
- If it's an appliance you're getting repaired, check the yellow pages for the dealer authorized to service your brand; he should be able to spot what's wrong quickly and will have the parts on hand to fix it.

The more things you can learn to do for yourself, the better. That goes for tuning the car, too, and for preparing your own income tax. I'm not saying that you have to *do* these things; you can also save time and hire someone, just as you can hire someone to do your housework. The important thing is just knowing that you *can* do things for yourself if you have to.

"When my husband left seven years ago, I was convinced that all my problems would be solved if I could get married again," says Linda, thirty-eight, divorced when her children were preschoolers. "Then, slowly, I learned that I could handle everything I had depended on him for. I found reliable child care, got a degree, and found a job in my field. And when the roof needed repair, I learned I had three viable options: I could fix it myself, call a repair person, or live with it. I feel in control of my life now and good about myself. Now, if I become involved in a relationship, I have a lot more going for me."

FOR RICHER OR FOR POORER

In many marriages, it is common for the man to take care of the major financial investments and the woman to balance the checkbook. But if you're suddenly on your own as a result of widowhood or divorce, you may be faced with handling large sums of money. In place of your monthly budget, you may find yourself with one sizable insurance or divorce settlement combined with a sharply reduced income.

Or perhaps, after years of scraping by on student loans or a subsidy from your parents, you have finally landed that hard-earned degree and a lucrative job. At last you will have money left over after meeting expenses, and you want to invest it where it will pay the highest interest.

Either way, you need to learn about things like municipal bonds, money-market certificates, estate planning, investment securities, and mutual funds.

Some of us are completely at ease in the world of high finance. And some of us freeze at the sight of any figure higher than three digits. Most handicapped of all are those of us—brought up on that risky notion that "someone will be around to take care of us"—who have had little exposure to money matters.

It's only as scary as it is unfamiliar. Stephanie Winston's *Getting Organized* contains a good section on basic budgeting. And Sylvia Porter's *Money Books* offer an easy-to-understand yet comprehensive overview of consumer economics.

If you're saying to yourself, "Investments?! I can barely keep up with the minimum payments on my BankAmericard," you need another kind of financial advice. A licensed credit-counseling service can help you develop a sound, workable budget and get you out of debt.

There are too many finance-related issues to cover in a few paragraphs: Your salary, fixed and flexible expenses, and even the area of the country in which you live have a big impact on what you can save or spend. The point is: Learn to handle money as if *you* are to be your one and everlasting means of support, because that may be the case. (You may someday even be in the position of supporting someone else!)

"A big test of how serious you are about your own independence is your attitude toward money," observes Vivian, divorced for ten years and raising two daughters. "Are you signed up for your company pension plan? Buying a house or a condominium? Watching the prime lending rate and the stock market? If you say you can't afford these investments, then what are you *planning* to do toward getting a better job at a higher income?

"Women, married or single, can't afford to leave financial matters to chance on the belief that someone will be around to 'take care of them.'"

Time management and money management are inseparable. It costs money to buy services that save time, to take that vacation that restores your energy and spirits. In short, money, prudently managed, helps us achieve our quality-of-life goals. You don't have to be rich—just solvent.

SINGLE MOTHERS HAVE IT ALL

If being single seems glamorous and motherhood is revered, then single mothers would seem to have it all. And do they ever—all the responsibility, all the work, all the conflicts. Yet their ranks are increasing, along with the divorce rate, and they are managing. Many single mothers, after the initial period of adjustment, would even report that they are prospering.

"Single mothers can't seem to help but put pressures on themselves," Vivian observes, "trying to be far-above-average listeners, disciplinarians, providers...because beneath it all, as a single parent, you feel guilty. After all, you feel at least partly responsible because your kids don't have a father.

"You set standards, at first, that are impossible to live up to. Something has to go, and for me it was my magazine image of Good Motherhood. My house didn't look like the pages of *Good Housekeeping*; my daughters were not carrying finger sandwiches and decorated carrot sticks to school in their lunch boxes. It has taken me years to get over feeling guilty about that."

The children—who make the aftermath of a divorce extra difficult—are also the ones who make life worthwhile, single mothers agree. Children stave off the loneliness and the feeling that "this was all for nothing." And the companionship between single parents and their children frequently evolves into a deep and enduring relationship.

But it's important, they add, to build support systems with other adults, and to avoid creating too much mutual dependence between themselves and their children.

Moving into a new community after her divorce, Marlene joined organizations related to her eight-year-old daughter's activities. Sitting on PTO committees and the day-camp governing board "wasn't the kind of social life I would choose permanently," she says, "but for a time, it served a real purpose. It was a good way of making contact with other single parents and couples."

"In the Unitarian church in our community, we have 'extended families' consisting of couples, grandparents, single adults, and children," relates Linda. "The group gives me legitimate access to a wide group of people instead of gravitating only to other divorced women my own age."

The last thing single mothers should do, these women agree, is to go it alone. Church groups, community colleges, a local community mental health center, and support groups such as Parents Without Partners can all put single mothers in touch with others in their situation with whom they can share problems and experience.

"There's no shame in getting professional help to see you through a crisis," one adds. "It helped me sort things out at a time when I needed someone thoroughly objective to turn to. I looked upon it very much like taking a course in myself."

BUT IT CAN BE LONELY

With so many demands on our time and so many choices, most of us put a premium on time that is ours alone. So I asked the women I surveyed, "If you had two totally free hours today, all to yourself, how would you spend them?"

"I have a whole evening stretching before me, tonight and every night, and I hate it!" one respondent shot back.

"Loneliness is debilitating," the woman, divorced two years ago, continued. "You just pace around, feeling at loose ends, unable to concentrate. You can drain all your energy, just feeling sorry for yourself. Talk about counterproductive!"

I spoke with some of my unmarried friends about loneliness and how they dealt with it. Here are some of their comments:

"If you are married, you have a built-in social life," Jeanne points out. "You have someone to talk to; someone who keeps up with your daily affairs. Someone to say on the spur of the moment, 'Let's go out for pizza.' Single, you face total responsibility for creating enjoyment in your life. If you used to clean house with your husband and sometimes looked forward to taking a break and sitting down with him with a glass of beer, now you're faced with a dirty house and a lot of guilt if you sit around drinking beer alone.

"One of my big fears when we decided to separate was losing that spontaneity of togetherness. I was in the shower brooding about this one evening when I got a phone call—my good friend Margo inviting me out to a movie," she says. "That call not only picked up my spirits at the time, but showed me that life would not be all that empty and predictable just because I was on my own again.

"One advantage to being single is that it frees you to develop much closer, more intimate friendships with other women and men," she adds. "Married, you may not have the time or inclination to pursue these relationships."

Similarly, time alone is an opportunity to get involved in new activities—plans you put aside because a former lover or spouse had no interest in them. "*Involved*" is a key word here, the women emphasized. It's not enough to simply be *occupied*.

Chris describes another side. "Living alone, it's harder to achieve a balance. With a full-time job and two demanding graduate math courses, I tend to get so absorbed in my work that everything else goes. My personal and social life can dwindle to nothing and I'm hardly aware of it. A husband or children pull you into their worlds and enlarge your sphere of interests. I tend to get a little skewed, and that's not healthy.

"Sure you catch yourself getting lonely sometimes," she adds, "but brooding doesn't help. You find constructive ways to deal with it. Call a friend. Turn on some good music. Write a letter to someone you care about. Get out of the apartment and be among people!"

"I find one of the best places to go is the gym," suggests Anne, thirty, who balances her long solitary weekends of writing fiction with late-afternoon four-mile runs. "I find if I'm consistent about doing the things I really like to do, I inevitably meet people of similar interests.

"A library is a nice comfortable place to go when you're lonesome," she adds. "It's a warm atmosphere with a low level of activity. It's free. And books respond to you, without demanding anything of you."

"I take myself to a nice restaurant," Chris says. "I know some people have a hang-up about eating alone, but for me it's an adventure. I like to discover new, interesting places. I may bring something with me to read, but if I'm in the mood, I just enjoy watching the people."

Being with people, the women agree, is not as important as establishing long-term, caring relationships. "I'll never forget one time when I was having lunch with my friend Myra, a woman in her seventies," Jeanne relates. "She looked at her watch and said, 'Louise must be back from the doctor's by now.' She jumped up and dialed her friend's number and without even saying hello asked her, 'Well, what did he say?' Each of us needs at least one special, supportive person in our lives. One person who cares what the doctor says."

Friends are a precious resource, for sounding out thoughts, sharing advice and experience, and sometimes just for companionship.

But most important of all, these single women conclude, is to be comfortable in your own company. On a moment-to-moment basis, you can't rely on other people to keep you entertained or motivated. They have their own lives to look after. As Ralph Waldo Emerson said, "Nothing can bring you peace but yourself."

Superwoman: R.I.P.

She can bring home the bacon, fry it up in the pan...and never let you forget you're a man. She's popping up repeatedly on television commercials lately, this sultry blonde swinging a briefcase in one hand and a skillet in the other. Advertisers were slow to acknowledge the career-woman/wife/mother, but once they discovered her, they signed her to promote products ranging from cosmetics to laundry detergents.

She's an improvement over those other women on television commercials who go around squeezing toilet paper and grieving over static cling. But many of us find her just as hard to relate to. She's so competent. She never looks mussed or harassed. As the camera pans over her gleaming kitchen, past her adoring husband and children, it is clear that her life is easy, perfect, and always under control.

The message we get from the media is, "Yes! Women *can* have it all! And we can handle it all!" (We can handle it even better with Sheer Energy pantyhose and Soup Starter soup mix, but the important thing is, it is within reach.) We can manage a stimulating job; well-adjusted children; a home worthy of a photo layout in *House Beautiful*; memorable little dinner parties, and an ecstatic sex life.

When "We *can* do it all" gives way to "We *must* do it all," we are caught in the Superwoman Syndrome.

It is a condition that particularly seems to afflict women in their late twenties to early thirties, as they attempt to mesh multiple roles. It can occur in the young homemaker who decides to go back to school or to work; in the established career woman having her first child; in the single woman who adds professional responsibilities at work and at the same time commits herself to two consulting contracts.

My mother calls it "spreading yourself too thin." Psychologists call it "role overload."

I see nothing wrong with taking on more than you're sure you can handle. How else can you test your limits? The pitfall is failure to continuously assess:

- What you are doing
- Why
- Where you can use shortcuts
- What you can eliminate

The Superwoman doesn't try to set priorities. She tries to do everything.

She tries to do it all *perfectly*: Top sales record in the company; cleanest house on the block. She takes her cue not only from the images she sees on the TV screen and in magazines, but from real-life acquaintances who seem to "have it all together."

She may assemble her role model by taking the best attributes of several friends. ("I've got to be as productive at work as Sylvia; as outstanding a cook as Barb.") And in not a few cases, her uncompromising standards are imposed by a magnanimous husband who says, "Sure you can get a job. As long as the house doesn't suffer."

Perhaps the most compelling reason we fall into the Superwoman snare is our difficulty in letting go of old roles as we add new ones. We especially cling to those we find truly gratifying. Cindy, who cared for my son for two years when I returned to work, is an example.

Raised in a Michigan farming community, Cindy, twenty-six, learned early to sew, knit, bake, can vegetables, and raise livestock. She was a one-person 4-H Club. Married at sixteen, with two sons at nineteen, she was determined to be the perfect wife and mother. To contribute her share financially, she became licensed to provide day-care services.

Cindy never had to advertise. Working mothers discovered her through word of mouth, and at one point her modest one-story home was bustling with two infants, two eighteen-month-olds, and three three-year-olds in addition to her own two sons, now aged six and eight. On school holidays she would welcome the older brothers and sisters of her charges, and even their friends. In a pinch, neighborhood mothers knew Cindy would make room for one more. She loved kids. And she hated to say no.

By now she was making pretty good money—an average of ten dollars per day from each of at least seven sets of parents. But she continued to sew her own clothes and bake nine loaves of bread every week from "force of habit." At Christmas she made a total of twenty-two stuffed animals for her growing clientele. To make sure her sons didn't feel lost in the crowd, she volunteered as room mother for both of the boys' classrooms and organized the school book fair. The March of Dimes discovered her and began priming her to chair the all-city fund raising campaign.

Had Cindy and her family not moved to a new city, I suspect she would have taken in more and more children and taken on more and more responsibilities indefinitely. She seemed to be caught in a tornado-like spiral of activity, too busy to pay attention to what she was trying to accomplish. "I was like one of our pet gerbils, running my legs off in a little wire wheel but not really getting anywhere," she says.

In the new community, Cindy took a hard look at her priorities and pared down her responsibilities to one job (as an insurance broker) and two children (her own). Sometimes it helps to make a clean break with the Superwoman Syndrome. But you can also work your way out gradually. Here are some easy steps, pulled from various previous chapters and assembled here for review.

1. *Make a list* of all your current roles and responsibilities—everything that makes a demand on your time and energy. Rank them twice: First according to how much time they take, and second, in order of their importance to you. Your list may look something like:

Roles	Hours per Week	Priority
Wife/lover }	25 to 40	1
Parent }		
Housekeeper	8	7
Employee	30	2
Classroom volunteer	4	8
Cook	8	6

Roles	Hours per Week	Priority
Laundress	4	9
Chauffeur	5	10
Choir member	7	5
Tennis player	3	4
Reader	6	3
Sleeper	49	6

The purpose of this exercise is to give you an idea where your times goes, and which of your lower priorities might be eliminated.

2. *Practice saying "no"* to new demands on your time. If you feel a sense of relief afterward instead of regret, you'll know you've done the right thing.

3. *Identify your support group*: Caring friends, relatives, and other associates with whom you can exchange services and pool resources.

4. *Ask for help*. Delegate responsibilities at home and at work (making sure that you're also extending privileges and rewards—not just dumping on people).

5. *Look for ways to cut corners*, focusing on results, not processes. A bakery cake is just as welcome as a home-baked one—and there are no bowls to clean up!

6. *Look for ways to simplify your life*. Some women I've interviewed suggested these moves:

- Cut commuting time by moving closer to your workplace
- Change your style of entertaining. Make everything potluck
- Hire a housekeeper
- Gift-shop by catalogue. Have everything wrapped and shipped direct from the store

Here's another consideration. "I was a nervous wreck under the pressures of a job I disliked and unreliable child care," says a mother whose daughters are aged one-and-a-half and three. "I quit, we sold the second car and cut back our standard of living. I have never regretted it."

7. *Make time for yourself*. Never allow yourself to become so driven that you sacrifice time to do what *you* most want—to sleep, read, run three miles, or simply relax and do nothing.

PROGNOSIS: FULL RECOVERY

The Superwoman Syndrome is temporary, not terminal. We are most vulnerable around our late twenties, I think, because by then we have accumulated many responsibilities and are still learning to strike a balance among them. Just as it is hard for most adolescents to handle the responsibilities of marriage and parenthood, it's hard for a twenty-seven-year-old to coordinate the complex demands of a job, a home, and child care. We're still getting to know ourselves. As Gail Sheehy writes in *Passages*:

> It is rarely possible for a woman to integrate marriage, career and motherhood in her twenties and it's about time some of us who have tried said so. It is quite possible at 30 and decidedly possible at 35, but before then, the *personal* integration necessary as ballast simply hasn't had a chance to develop. In conversations with Margaret Mead and Daniel Levinson, I found both agreed.[1]

As we move through our thirties, several things begin to work in our favor. We become more competent and at ease in our jobs. Our children, past the diaper stage, grow more self-reliant. Our priorities, although still evolving, become more clear, and simply because we have had more years of practice, we're better able to handle them. In many cases our income is higher, so we can pay other people to perform services we formerly handled alone. Finally, we grow more secure in our personal relationships and more comfortable with ourselves.

This dichotomy was well represented at a university workshop I attended on "The Superwoman Myth." The participants included women who were living the part: One had just had a baby and was launching her own business; a mother of seven (including four adopted) children, recently divorced, was completing a degree in social work.

Several others were women in their mid-twenties, most of them just completing degrees or starting well-paying jobs, who were already experiencing doubts about whether they could ever have children or even be married and pursue their chosen careers.

[1]Gail Sheehy, *Passages* (New York: E. P. Dutton and Company, Inc.), p. 277.

Sandra, twenty-six, who is completing an M.B.A. in marketing and interviewing with several large corporations, remarked, "I'm glad I'm single and mobile enough to settle anywhere. I see marriage as a real handicap. If I were offered a great chance for advancement in one part of the country and my husband had a promising opportunity in another, who would make the sacrifice? Children are another dilemma. Will it hurt my career if I take time off to have a baby? Will I be too old to have one by the time I'm ready? I don't want to become a narrow-minded, self-centered person, absorbed only in my work. Yet I don't want to be overextended and then fail at everything."

At the other end of the spectrum were the women whose choices had already been made. Mickey, forty-three, who has eleven- and twelve-year-old children and a job in guidance and counseling, observes that "It's hard to see parenthood or career as an either/or proposition once you're into them. I can't imagine giving up either my children or my career. For me, the issue is learning to strike a balance."

Feminist author Letty Cottin Pogrebin writes this about the enigma of "having it all":

> We have discovered from each other's experiences that *none* of us has it all in society's eyes or in our own. The woman with a loving husband, three children, a successful career, an activist commitment, and a teaching job one night a week feels driven and compulsive and inadequate to the Everything she's supposed to be enjoying. The single woman with a career plan, free-flowing personal life, and economic self-sufficiency feels the Everything she has is diminished because she's only a one-ball juggler in a world that expects a three-ball circus act.
>
> The single mother, the poor mother, the unemployed woman, the older woman laboring in an unglamorous job with no time left for a "life plan"—where does she plug into the Everything ethic?[2]

Sally, thirty-six, who recently started her first job after being separated from her husband, and is thinking about graduate school but not until her children are older and more independent, observes astutely, "Our lives are pretty long. We don't *have* to have a baby, establish a career, and run for City Council all simultaneously. We can space out our ambitions over a period of many decades."

[2]Letty Cottin Pogrebin, "Can Women Really Have It All?...Should We?" *Ms.*, March 1978, p. 48.

How right she is. The Women's Movement has expanded our choices. But by choosing to do everything—right now, perfectly—we don't improve our position much. We are just as trapped, and twice as exhausted.

The key to managing multiple roles, whether as a single independent career woman, a working wife and mother or, hardest of all, a single parent, is flexibility and compromise. Know your values and carefully channel your energy into those areas which offer you the greatest psychic rewards. Remember, you don't have to do it all, and you don't have to do it alone.

You can have your cake and eat it too. But don't always insist on baking it from scratch. And get someone to help you sweep up the crumbs.

Appendix

PERSONAL TIME TACTICS

Write down goals: For the next six months and the next three years. Review them regularly. Ask yourself what you've done lately to help yourself achieve them.

Keep a list. Write down what you have to do; establish priorities; do things in order of importance.

Use a daily-planning calendar to record all appointments, social activities, birthdays, and other personal reminders. Don't just note business that involves other people; block off time for your own priorities and commitments.

Plan your day for a few minutes each morning and review, at the end of the day, what went well and what could be improved.

Continuously reassess your priorities. Ask yourself, "Is this the best possible use of my time at this moment?" If it isn't...

Be flexible. Your "To-Do" list is a guideline, not iron law. If a summer hailstorm sabotages your intended activities for the day, shift to Plan B with a free spirit.

Follow your energy cycle. Do difficult, important tasks during the time of day you feel peppy and alert; save mindless routine chores for when your energy level is lower.

Push yourself, or you'll never find out how much you can get done. When you sense you are becoming overextended, weed out activities of lowest priority. That way you'll constantly upgrade your accomplishments.

If it's quick, do it now. An invoice comes in for your signature, a button pops off, your child asks for help fixing a toy; naturally you don't welcome the interruption, but taking care of the matter immediately may take less time then remembering to do it later.

If you tend to procrastinate:

Ease in. Just beginning a task gives you some momentum and makes the end result look more manageable.
Block out time for your task and stick to it. Finish all you can within the time frame.
Do the worst first.
Make a commitment to someone to finish by a certain deadline.
Promise yourself a reward.

Don't be perfectionist. Unless you're part of a trapeze act, just shoot for excellence.

Designate a family message center, using a bulletin board or blackboard near the telephone, or refrigerator magnets.

Do everything in the off hours. Shift your work schedule, if possible, in order to hit 'the roads when the traffic is not heavy, restaurants when they're not crowded, stores when they aren't busy.

Get up an hour earlier. You can get a jump on the day, have a relaxed breakfast, exercise, get some work done while the house is quiet, or run a few errands on the way to the office.

If you're often running late, try working backwards. Envision your goal, the steps it will take to reach it, and how long each of them will take. Now you know how much time to allow before your deadline.

Make time for yourself. At least twice a week, take time off from whatever you're doing for other people and spend at least an hour on what *you* want to do. Schedule the hour in. Rank it among your prime commitments.

OFFICE HOURS

Separate the responsibilities of job and family. Neither update your grocery list at the office nor bring a loaded briefcase home. If your office is *in* your home, designate a specific work space and keep regular hours there.

Set specific, realistic objectives for the next hour, the day, the week. View your agenda in terms of what *must* be done and why; what you would like to do; and what you should skip or delegate.

Reserve blocks of time for jobs that require intense concentration, and avoid interruptions. Finish routine tasks when the office is noisy or distracting.

Unclutter your desk of everything but work in progress. Sort the papers into a vertical stacking file. Move photos, plants, and homey knickknacks to a shelf where they are not a distraction.

Keep fewer files with broader categories. Save only those things you're sure you'll need for future reference. If uncertain, store the item for six months in the bottom drawer.

Never handle paperwork more than twice, once to read it and once to take action. In between, stow it in a bring-up file labeled for the date when action must be taken.

To minimize interruptions, look politely at the visitor, but as if you have been interrupted. Keep your pen in your hand. Lean forward in your chair. Or stand. Don't invite the interrupter to sit down.

Schedule meetings close to lunch or quitting time, to discourage participants from pursuing irrelevant discussions. Always start on time, follow an agenda, and summarize to the group, before it disbands, what you feel has been accomplished.

Discuss your ambitions with your boss. Ask for a performance review. Discuss career ladders, raises, training programs. Volunteer for new responsibilities that fit in with your career goals.

Talk positively among your male colleagues. Don't complain about child-care hassles, discrimination, and other such matters. Hide your harassed side. Instead, let them see how well you cope.

Hire the best people you can. Their competence will make your job easier and reflect credit on your judgement.

Delegate as many tasks as possible to your subordinates, giving them the authority and recognition that go with the new responsibilities. Free yourself to take on bigger things.

Network with other successful, influential women and men both within and outside your organization. Use your connections to get information and assistance when appropriate. Feel equally free to grant favors in return.

Avoid business lunches. They tend to stretch a twenty-minute transaction into two hours of stuffing and socializing, breaking your momentum for afternoon tasks.

Take a break. Take a walk, clear your head, do something diverting. You'll be gaining time, not losing it, by reviving your energy and spirit.

If you work from your home, section off, for your business, a space that is separate from the rest of the house, even if it's only a desk or a table that is for your use alone. Keep a separate business checkbook, file system, account books, and other essential items.

On business air travel, try to consolidate your belongings in a hanging garment bag you can carry on board. Always hand-carry important papers, money, jewelry, and one copy of any hand-outs you've checked through with luggage. If the luggage is delayed, you can still make extra copies before a presentation.

HOUSEWORK

First, go for the clutter. The house will be more maneuverable and restful if the dishes are put away, surfaces cleared, newspapers picked up, and other such tasks done.

For the mass cleanup, start with a different room each time, so that none gets totally neglected.

Pick up a mess as you generate it; the more it accumulates, the more depressing it becomes and the more complicated the cleanup.

Don't adhere to a schedule (Monday: laundry; Tuesday: baking; and so on). Be flexible, and do things according to necessity, not rigid routine.

Set the timer. Since housework has a way of taking as much time as you decide to allocate to it, make a game of seeing how much you can get done within fifteen or thirty minutes.

Buy a new cleaning agent, a new mop head, or a wiry scrubbing brush. A new tool may give you an added incentive to get to work, and may also speed the job along.

Consolidate cleaning supplies in a carry-all container. Group the tools you use at the same time—paper towels with the glass-cleaner; the detergent and scrub brush in the pail. Store them in or near the rooms they'll be used in—a set for each floor.

When hand-washing dishes, pour soap directly on the washrag or sponge, soap the dishes, stack them in the sink, rinse them in very hot water, and stack them in the dish drainer to dry.

Install (locking) casters on large pieces of furniture so that they may be moved easily for vacuuming.

When you redecorate, choose easy-to-clean wall and floor coverings: Enamel rather than flat paint; vinyl wallpaper; wood paneling; corkboard; no-wax linoleum; tile; heather-toned carpeting.

Throw things away. Empty your drawers and closets and simplify your life. Recycle what's salvable in a garage sale or bundle it all up for a local charity or thrift shop. Get a receipt; most donations are tax deductible.

Involve everyone in the household in big cleaning projects and day-to-day maintenance. Emphasize that everybody pitches in because everybody benefits. Let each person pick the job they prefer or do best; rotate the rest of the work.

Hire help and don't feel guilty or extravagant. "Having a maid has freed our family to explore the Boston area and attend educational and cultural events," says Jan, on a graduate fellowship at Harvard. "We would not have had such experiences if we spent every weekend cleaning house together."

In the living room, keep a large basket handy for fast pick-ups. Baskets and bins are also useful for collecting mittens and boots, toddler's toys, the week's newspapers, and many other kinds of loosely associated objects.

To clean the bathroom fast, run hot water in the shower for five minutes to steam up the tile walls and porcelain. Then just wipe them down with a sponge or paper towels.

The bathroom rule: Leave everything as you find it. If each family member straightens his or her towel, rinses and replaces the soap, swishes out the sink, and sponges the toilet, the room will remain spotless.

Own a sewing machine for simple mending and alterations, even if you don't plan to construct a wardrobe with it.

Organize children's rooms so that the children can care for their own things. Toddlers need a low closet rod, dresser drawers within reach, a few shelves to display special toys, and containers of all sizes for organizing crayons, puzzle pieces, blocks, and other items. Speed bedmaking by using a European-style quilt or a slumber bag.

To induce children to take care of their rooms, let them choose their own paint color and curtain and bedspread fabric. They may take more interest in cleaning if they get to decorate.

LAUNDRY

Don't designate an entire day for doing laundry; fit it into the "cracks" in the day. Load the machine at night, run it when you get up, put the wash in the dryer as you leave for work, and put it away when you get home.

Let polyester-blend clothing drip-dry on hangers over the shower rod instead of rushing it out of the dryer to avoid wrinkles.

Eliminate sorting by using a system of several clothes hampers: One for dark items, one for light, one for permanent press.

Or, have everyone toss underwear and towels directly into the washing machine. Run a load when the machine is full; do other types of wash as necessary.

Or, use a different hamper for each family member. Each person over the age of eight does his or her own laundry. This also eliminates sorting and redistributing afterward.

Douse stained or soiled clothing with soap after taking it off instead of making a special inspection before washing.

Buy all socks of the same color. Share them, in one community sock drawer, among family members having similar-sized feet.

Or, pin socks together before putting them into the wash, instead of searching for matching pairs afterward.

Pick a laundromat within or near a shopping area so you can buy groceries, run errands, etc., while the clothes are being washed.

FAST FOOD

Don't go grocery shopping more than once a week. To cut the time further:

- Settle on one store that offers quality and proximity, and learn its layout. Chasing specials all over town costs more time than it saves in cash.
- Always take a list and stick to it.
- Avoid the rush hours of 5:30 to 7 P.M. on weekdays and 10 A.M. to noon on Saturdays.
- Obtain a check-cashing card to speed check approval.
- Bag your own groceries.

For faster menu planning, map out a list of the staples your family always uses, group them in the order of their location in the store, and mimeograph the list. Checking off the needed items will take less time than having to rethink of them each time.

Post a grocery list in the kitchen, where each family member can note items that are due to run out.

Stockpile easy family favorites such as frozen pizza, breakfast bars, canned ravioli, macaroni and cheese—anything that can supply sustenance in a rush.

Prepare multiple amounts of a cooked dish and freeze meal-sized portions for later use.

Make a large roast, ham, or turkey, and serve variations during the week; or freeze big hunks of the meat for later use. Freeze cooked meats in broth to extend their shelf life and reduce the chance of freezer burn.

Double the size of at least one side-dish. Plan a big pot of rice, tossed salad, or vegetables to last through two meals.

Store leftovers in pots in which they can be heated, or in bowls in which they can be served.

Make lunchbox sandwiches for the full week and freeze them; they'll thaw out by noon. Assemble cookies, potato chips, and other lunch snacks in plastic bags the night before; put a thermos of cold beverage in the freezer.

Hang up the pots, pans, and kitchen tools you use most often on an accessible rack—right after you've washed them. You'll save search time and storage space.

Take advantage of time savers like automatic turn-on ovens, crock pots, food processors, pressure cookers, and microwave ovens. At the same time...

Don't accumulate dozens of single-use appliances such as hot-dog roasters and donut makers unless they really earn their keep. A good rule for any gadget is: If you haven't used it in a year, pass it on to someone who will.

Take the family out to a restaurant when you're pressed for time. A take-out pizza, fish, or chicken costs only a couple of dollars more than your home-cooked fare and saves you at least an hour of cooking and cleanup. Your time is worth that many times over.

QUALITY TIME

With your children: Spend time alone each day with each of them, no matter what. Pick a quiet time when there are no distractions, perhaps a few minutes at bedtime.

With your husband: Plan a late, simple-but-elegant dinner after the kids are in bed. Dress up, light candles, turn on music. Don't talk about money.

If communications break down, try a family meeting. Adults and children get a chance to air grievances, resolve differences, revise the duty roster, and perhaps plan an outing together.

Assign chores to children that are a learning experience and a help to you—not just busywork.

Foster independence. The more self-reliant your children become, the better for all of you. At as early an age as possible, teach them to ride the bus, dial emergency phone numbers, assist with housework, and prepare simple foods.

COMPANY COMING

Keep a small stockpile of special foods on hand for unexpected guests: A crock of cheese, some bottles of wine, assorted crackers, frozen egg rolls and pizza, and a pie shell that can be filled with fresh fruit and ice cream.

Don't invite one couple to dinner; invite three. It's as easy to prepare dishes for eight people as four, and you're under less pressure because while you're in the kitchen, your friends entertain one another.

Give parties back-to-back. Invite one set of acquaintances for cocktails on Saturday, another group for Sunday brunch. Then, the house only has to be cleaned once, and many of the dishes can be adapted to either menu.

Hire neighborhood teenagers to help with parties. They can help tend bar, bus dishes, entertain children, and assist with the cleanup.

Accept help. When a guest asks, "What can I bring?" suggest a simple appetizer or a bottle of wine. Reciprocate.

Keep it simple. Organize a picnic or a pot-luck party, or meet at a Chinese restaurant. Or skip the emphasis on food and get together for a play, concert, or sports event.

STRATEGIC SHOPPING

Familiarity breeds speed. As with the supermarket, choose a department or discount store that offers quality and convenience. Learn when sales are scheduled and which brands suit you the best.

Shop when the stores are least crowded. This tends to be before 11:30 A.M., in midafternoon, in late evening, and any time it's rainy.

Shop purposefully instead of on impulse. In the spring and fall, take inventory of the clothes you own and what colors and items you need to update or fill out your wardrobe. Do the same for your children's clothes. Buy socks, underwear, cotton turtlenecks, and other such items by catalogue.

Use the phone to comparison shop and to make sure that the merchants have in stock what you need. When you decide on an item, ask the store if they can set it aside or deliver it.

Keep all receipts in a drawer or shoe box. Weed them out occasionally, but keep most for six months. One woman got a replacement pair of shoes after arguing successfully that forty-dollar sandals should hold up for more than one summer.

Order gifts from catalogues and have them mailed direct, saving time and the cost of two mailings.

Pick out one great gift and give variations of it to everybody.

Fill a basket with foods from a specialty shop: Imported delicacies; wine; cheese and crackers; picnic items. This makes a great gift for anyone on your list, from newlyweds to grandparents.

Don't wait until December: Shop for gifts all year. Buy the "perfect gift" when you see it and stash it away until the birthday or Christmas. If you have a toddler, keep a small supply of children's gifts on hand for parties and other occasions. Let older children select their own gifts for their friends.

Buy greeting cards, wrapping paper, and ribbons in bulk so that you don't have to make a special trip when the occasion arrives.

Answer mail promptly. Address the envelope first. Tuck in notes, news clippings, and other items of interest. As the envelope fills, you'll feel more motivated to write the letter itself, and to get it in the mail.

TAMING THE TELEPHONE

Make all phone calls at one time instead of sporadically. Place the phone on the left side of the desk (if you are right handed) so you can take notes as you speak. If you type, get a phone with a shoulder rest.

Whenever you look up a phone number you expect to use more than once, circle it in the phone book so it will be easier to spot next time.

Organize your phone contacts in an indexed three-by-five-inch card file. Turn sideways the cards for persons you need to call or expect a return call from. The upturned cards "flag" your attention to those people you need to contact.

Prominently post a list of phone numbers you use often or may need in an emergency, such as those of the police, fire departments, the ambulance, relatives, and babysitters. Keep a pad of paper or chalkboard nearby for messages.

Don't feel locked-in to a call that comes at an inconvenient time; arrange to call back later. Give your friends the same courtesy. If your call will take more than two minutes, ask immediately if you've picked a bad time and offer to call later.

An answering service or recorded-message machine can allow you to return calls at your convenience instead of someone else's.

Resolve conflicts over phone use with teenagers by agreeing on a time limit. Use a kitchen timer to enforce it. Or install a second telephone and let them pay for it.

In the kitchen, choose a wall phone with a long cord and shoulder rest so you can continue scraping dishes or preparing meals while talking. Keep mending or other busywork near the phone if you're often trapped in long conversations. Or do calisthenics for the duration of the call.

NIGGLING DETAILS

Pile items to be returned or delivered, into the car as soon as you're through with them, as a reminder to drop them off and to keep them from getting lost in the house.

Combine errands. Never make a special trip just to the dry cleaners; swing by the bank, library, and repair shop as well. Make a list of your stops and mentally map out your route before starting.

Pay bills and balance the checkbook once a month instead of intermittently when the bills come in.

Save the traveler's checks left over from your vacation; they can spare you an emergency trip to the bank.

Enter checks for tax-deductible expenses with a red felt-tip pen so that they'll be easy to sort out at tax time.

Keep your packing lists from vacations and business trips. Why rethink all those items from one trip to the next? File your lists of necessities for business conferences, ski weekends, and other trips in a "Travel" file, along with maps and brochures.

Schedule doctor's appointments at the beginning of the day so that you can be in and out before the doctor gets behind. Or call before you leave for an appointment to see if they're behind schedule. If they are, adjust your departure time or bring a supply of work to do while you're waiting.

Bring along things to do, a pen and stationery, a book to read, knitting yarn, or something else if you're frequently waiting for others. While standing in lines or sitting in waiting rooms, update your "To-Do" list.

Post a large wall calendar with plenty of space around each date for recording anniversaries, appointments, school holidays, and other events. Each family member should also mark his or her own activities on this, both as a reminder and to prevent conflicts.

FEELING TERRIFIC

Exercise may seem to expend energy but it actually increases it. It releases tension, builds stamina, and improves the quality of your sleep. For optimum results, combine aerobic (high-exertion) exercise for your heart and lungs with calisthenics for strength and muscle tone.

Fit exercise into your daily routine by taking the stairs instead of the elevator. Walk or bike to work, or if you must drive, park far from your destination. Mow your own lawn and do your own heavy housework.

Take excellent care of yourself. Once a year, have a physical and Pap smear. Twice a year, see the dentist. Once a month, examine your breasts. Daily, get enough sleep, nutrition, and exercise so that every day is lived, not lived through.

Get enough sleep. Some people drag through the day on a chronic sleep deficit. They feel muddled and overworked, yet keep "burning the midnight oil" in an attempt to catch up. Well rested, they could accomplish lots more in less time.

FOR APPEARANCE'S SAKE

Settle on an easy-care, wash-and-wear hairdo that doesn't require fussing or setting. Buy a blow-dryer, curling iron, or whatever else you need to keep maintenance time to a minimum.

Practice applying makeup until you can do it in seconds.

Keep cosmetics to a minimum. Light lipstick, a little liquid make-up or powder, needs less frequent touch-up. Clear nailpolish is less noticeable when chipped. Brush-on blushers and shadows can be applied faster than cream-types and you don't have to wash your fingers.

Lay clothes out the night before you're going to wear them so you don't have to go off on a frantic morning search for a matching belt or a missing button. Do the same with children's outfits.

Take clothes to the dry cleaner promptly so you're not caught with "nothing to wear." Keep up with laundry and ironing for the same reason.

TWO FOR THE PRICE OF ONE

Television rarely deserves undivided attention. Read the program guide and plan your viewing selectively (and insist that your kids do likewise). Then:

Save all mindless tasks such as ironing, clipping coupons, and straightening drawers for doing during the chosen program.

Keep a project box of toys to be repaired, clothing to be mended, and crafts-in-progress. Consolidate the tools (needle and thread, ceramic glue, other items) in the same box so that they're handy even when you sit down for a fifteen-minute newscast.

Use commuting time to catch up on reading, write letters, and use a dictating machine. If you're driving, it's a good time to plan your day (or review it on the way home and set goals for tomorrow).

Read the newspaper while watching the news telecast. Use the commentator's brief synopsis as an index to the stories you want to read about in more detail.

While talking on the phone do leg exercises, file your nails, pet the dog.

In the shower, do your hand-washing.

Convert routine tasks into quality time with your kids. When you must take preschoolers along on an errand, call it an "adventure." Point out landmarks and interesting sights. At the grocery store, teach older children to read unit prices and select fresh meats and produce. Use the times when you're driving, working, or eating together to catch up on news and discuss problems. Above all, keep the lines of communication open.

FINALLY

Keep your spirits up. Worrying, brooding, and feeling guilty are a drain on both your psychic and your physical energy. If something is bugging you, don't let it fester; take action or firmly turn your attention to the positive side of things. Stay optimistic. Your state of mind is probably the most important factor in how effectively you get things accomplished.

RECOMMENDED READING

Time Management

BLISS, EDWIN C. *Getting Things Done.* New York: Charles Scribner's Sons. 1976.

BLISS, EDWIN C. *Doing it Now.* New York: Charles Scribner's Sons. 1983.

FERNER, JACK D. *Successful Time Management.* New York: John Wiley and Sons. 1980.

GOLDFEIN, DONNA. *Every Woman's Guide To Time Management.* Les Femmes. 1977.

JANUZ, LAUREN R. and MAGON, KIM M. *Using Time Management to Get More Done.* Smith Collins. 1992.

KNAUS, WILLIAM J. *Do It Now.* New York: Prentice Hall Press. 1979.

LAKEIN, ALAN. *How to Get Control of Your Time and Your Life.* New York: Wyden. 1973.

LEBOEUF, MICHAEL. *Working Smart.* New York: McGraw-Hill Book Co. 1979.

MACKENZIE, R. ALEX. *The Time Trap.* New York: McGraw-Hill Book Co. 1975.

SCOTT, DRU. *How To Put More Time In Your Life.* New York: Signet. 1981.

Getting Organized

EVATT, CHRISLYNNE. *How to Organize Your Closet ... And Your Life.* Ballentine. 1981.

WINSTON, STEPHANIE. *Getting Organized.* New York: Warner Books. 1978.

WINSTON, STEPHANIE. *The Organized Executive.* New York: Warner Books. 1983.

Parenting

DINKMEYER, DON A. and McKAY, GARY D. *Raising a Responsible Child.* New York: Simon and Schuster. 1973.

GINOTT, HAIM. Between Parent and Child. New York: Macmillan. 1965.

GORDON, THOMAS. *P.E.T. Parent Effectiveness Training.* New York: Wyden Books. 1970.

Housework

ASLETT, DON. *Is There Life After Housework?* Cincinnati, OH: Writer's Digest Books. 1981.

BRACKEN, PEG. *The I Hate To Housekeep Book.* New York: Harcourt Brace and World Knight. 1962.

CONRAN, SHIRLEY. *Superwoman.* New York: Crown Publishers, Inc. 1978.

Personal Effectiveness

COVEY, STEPHEN R. *The 7 Habits of Highly Effective People.* New York: Fireside. 1990.

HARRIGAN, BETTY LEHAN. *Games Mother Never Taught You.* New York: Rawson Associates Publishers, Inc. 1977.

HENNING, MARGARET and JARDIM, ANNE. *The Managerial Woman.* New York: Doubleday. 1976.

LLOYD, KATE RAND, Ed. *The Working Woman Success Book.* New York: Ace Books. 1981.

Index